BMC 1100 and 1300

An Enthusiast's Guide

BMC 1100 and 1300

An Enthusiast's Guide

James Taylor

THE CROWOOD PRESS

First published in 2015 by
The Crowood Press Ltd
Ramsbury, Marlborough
Wiltshire SN8 2HR

www.crowood.com

British Library Cataloguing-in-Publication Data
A catalogue record for this book is available from the British Library.

ISBN 978 1 84797 989 6

Typeset and designed by D & N Publishing, Baydon, Wiltshire.

Printed and bound in Malaysia by Times Offset (M) Sdn Bhd.

CONTENTS

INTRODUCTION AND ACKNOWLEDGEMENTS

It is sad that a car which was so central to the motoring scene in Britain in the 1960s and 1970s has been so largely forgotten. The BMC 1100s and 1300s were everywhere in those years, doing stalwart if unspectacular service as family transport, and there will be many people who still remember them fondly.

For anyone with a serious interest in these cars, membership of The 1100 Club is essential. Formed in 1985, the club provides advice and support on all areas of owning and enjoying these cars as classics today. A first port of call should be the website at www.the1100club.com. In 2012 the club also published a delightful scrapbook of 1100 and 1300 material, *The Story of the BMC 1100*, which is very much worth the attention of any enthusiast.

A lot of people contributed to the present book, many of them without knowing they were doing so. I suppose this list should begin with my schoolfriend Chris's parents, who had a blue 1100 that he eventually ran into a ditch. They go on to include dozens of people in the old-car scene over a period of about forty years, and in particular I should single out a number of people who gave up their time at classic car shows to talk to me about their 1100s or 1300s, and willingly allowed me to photograph them as well.

Further photographs and material have come from my own collection, from the David Hodges Collection, from my friend Richard Bryant, from Glenn Smith in Australia, and from the archives of the Heritage Motor Centre. Special thanks also go to Magic Car Pics for photographic material, and to Barry Priestman of the Crayford Convertible Club for information and pictures from the club's archives. To all those I have not had the space to name or the wit to remember, sincere apologies – and thank you, too.

James Taylor
Oxfordshire
December 2014

CHAPTER ONE

ADO16: DESIGN, DEVELOPMENT AND OVERVIEW

The BMC 1100 and 1300 model range was one of the most successful in the Corporation's history, selling more than 2.1 million of all types between its introduction in 1962 and its demise in 1974. Worldwide, it was sold under eight different marque names and in two-door saloon, four-door saloon, two-door estate and five-door hatchback forms – and very nearly as a van as well. In Britain, it was the country's best-selling car between 1962 and 1971, being beaten just once (in 1967) by the Ford Cortina.

Yet even though the 1100s and 1300s were technological pioneers in their time, they are rare at classic car gatherings today. One reason is certainly that they were built at a time when rust-proofing was almost non-existent on British cars, so that thousands upon thousands of these cars simply rotted away to a point where repairs were no longer viable. Another must be that they were deliberately designed as practical and unglamorous family cars, with no sporting pretensions (although the 1300GT can perhaps be considered an honourable exception), so that there was little to persuade enthusiasts to keep them alive. Finally, perhaps, familiarity bred contempt: there were simply so many of them that they tended to blend into the background.

In fact, the ADO16 range, as it was known to its manufacturers, was a significant engineering achievement of its time, and confirmed BMC as a pioneer of new automotive ideas that had a profound impact on other manufacturers. The saddest part of the ADO16 story is that when British Leyland inherited this excellent product, it was either unable or unwilling to build upon it, and instead created bland, unadventurous and frequently unreliable replacements that eventually made it the butt of every TV comedian's jokes.

ORIGINS

To understand where the ADO16 models came from, we really have to trace the story back to 1952. That was the year when the two giants of the British motor industry, Austin and Morris, agreed to a merger under the umbrella title of the British Motor Corporation. This merger of rivals brought with it several subsidiary marques that had been acquired by the two organizations over the years – MG, Riley and Wolseley being the main car brands – and it also brought with it a number of problems. All of those marques had established strong dealer bodies, and those dealers had mostly established loyal customer bases. So there was considerable resistance below the surface to this attempt at unification: Riley dealers did not want to sell MGs, and Morris dealers did not want to sell Austins.

One aim of the BMC merger had been to make manufacturing savings by reducing the number of different models being built. There was no point, for example, in building completely different MG and Riley models when the two were actually competing for the same group of customers. So BMC responded to the problem with what is today often derisively described as 'badge-engineering'. That meant creating one basic design but producing different variants of it with different badges to suit the different dealer chains. The ADO16 models were born into that period, and that was why there were so many different versions of what was really one car. In the UK, they carried no fewer than six different marque badges – Austin, MG, Morris, Riley, Vanden Plas and Wolseley – and outside the UK they carried a couple more as well.

For its first few years, BMC continued to build and sell most of the models it had inherited from the Austin and Morris groups. Some still had plenty of life left in them and in any case developing new models takes time. But by 1955, BMC's Chairman, Leonard Lord (formerly the Austin Chairman), had embarked on a plan to rationalize the product range. He foresaw three basic models as the heart of the BMC car range, and they could wear whatever badges seemed appropriate at the time. There would be a large car, codenamed XC9001, a medium-sized car, XC9002, and a small car, XC9003.

Lord also wanted a talented engineer to lead the design teams, and his choice fell on Alec Issigonis. Issigonis had been responsible at Morris for the 1948 Morris Minor, a remarkable car that had completely outshone its Austin rivals, but he had sensed trouble when BMC was formed in 1952 and had left to work for Alvis. Here, Issigonis had designed an advanced new saloon car with an all-aluminium V8 engine, but sadly Alvis could not afford to put it into production. Lord recruited Issigonis for BMC and put him to work on the two larger car projects, XC9001 and XC9002.

It is the XC9002 that has most relevance to the ADO16 story, although it started life as a very different car. This was the medium-sized saloon, which at that stage had conventional rear-wheel drive and was intended as the eventual replacement for the Austin A40 and Morris Minor. However, work on the initial design was halted in early 1957 when Leonard Lord told Issigonis to abandon what he was doing and focus on the XC9003 small car.

What had happened was that petrol rationing had hit Britain in 1956, when some overseas governments had withdrawn supplies in protest

Alec Issigonis was the brilliant and innovative designer behind all BMC's front-wheel drive cars of the 1960s: the Mini, the 1100 and the 1800. In the late 1940s he had also designed the much-loved Morris Minor.

Leonard Lord was not a man to be trifled with; what he wanted, he got, and the 1100 range was part of his mid-1950s plan for a unified range of advanced BMC cars.

The first of Issigonis's designs for BMC was the Mini, which pioneered his space-saving packaging ideas when it was released in 1959.

against Britain's invasion of the Suez Canal zone. The political events that led to that need no discussion here, but one result was that cars that used as little petrol as possible were in demand. A number of entrepreneurs capitalized on the fact by importing miniature cars from the European continent. Bubble-cars and the like became big business, and the major UK manufacturers had nothing with which they could compete. Lord intended that BMC should compete – and fast.

Issigonis designed the new small car, which became the Mini on its 1959 announcement, around the need to obtain maximum interior space with minimum exterior dimensions. To that end, he designed a transverse powertrain, with the engine mounted across the front of the car and the gearbox mounted in the sump below it, driving the front wheels. It was a hugely effective solution, and so it was no surprise that he returned to it when he was allowed to start work again on the new medium-sized car, which was still known as XC9002.

His objective this time was to squeeze the interior dimensions of the latest BMC 1.5-litre saloons

This cutaway display model shows the side radiator arrangement, with air vents in the inner wing. To the right of it is one of the Hydrolastic suspension displacer units.

(the so-called Farina range) into the external dimensions of the Morris Minor, and the transverse powertrain packaging of the Mini enabled him to do this. Even with the wheels moved to the four

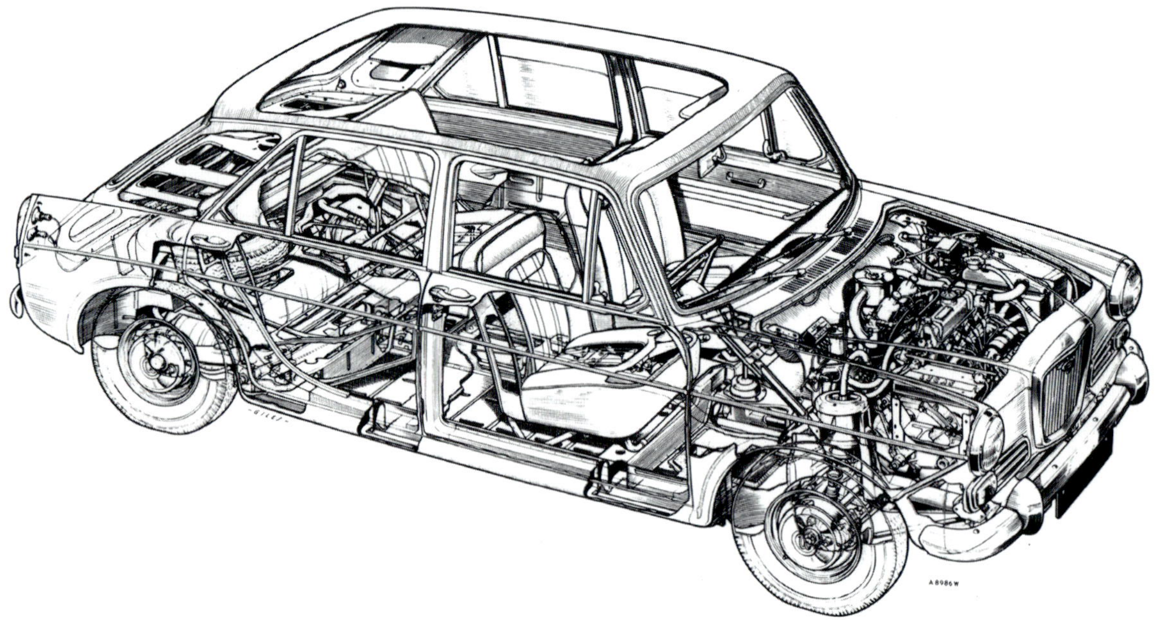

The overall layout of the ADO16 is shown in this cutaway drawing of a Wolseley 1100, with twin-carburettor engine.

corners of the car to give the long wheelbase that would give maximum ride comfort, XC9002 still had a wheelbase that was six inches shorter than that of the Farina saloons. With minimal front and rear overhangs, it ended up very much shorter overall than those cars, and at the time represented an absolute revolution in packaging.

Like the Mini, XC9002 was also going to have wheels that were much smaller than was then normal: in this case with a 12-inch diameter rather than the tiny 10-inch size used on the Mini. Issigonis made sure that there would be no compromises in ride comfort by engaging suspension specialist Alex Moulton as a consultant to BMC to work on the new car. Moulton had worked with Issigonis at Alvis and was a proponent of hydraulic suspension systems. It would be his Hydrolastic system that would be yet another innovation for BMC's new medium-sized car when it was announced in 1962 – and the same system would go on to be used on the Mini three years later. With all these elements in the design, the first prototypes of XC9002 were constructed and began trials during 1958.

THE PININFARINA INVOLVEMENT

Leonard Lord, meanwhile, was not at all convinced that his existing designers – 'stylists', as they were called at the time – could come up with convincingly modern shapes for the cars he wanted. So in 1957 he turned to the Italian styling house of Pininfarina and requested a range of new designs that would cover all the planned new BMC models. The first to reach the showrooms was the Austin A40, with characteristically sharp Italian lines. Next came the medium-sized designs, the so-called Farina cars, which really introduced BMC's badge engineering concept when they appeared with minor variations wearing the badges of the Austin, MG, Morris, Riley and Wolseley companies. The Mini, under development in this period, nevertheless escaped the attentions of Pininfarina, largely because of the rush to get it into production.

In the meantime, the early prototypes of XC9002 had been constructed with a simple and functional body design. This was distinctly dowdy and Lord

RIGHT: **Representing old-school engineering, but with modern Italianate styling by Pininfarina, this was the Austin A40.**

BELOW: **Pininfarina also drew up the shape of the conventionally engineered Austin A55, which introduced BMC's 'badge-engineering' to the world when it appeared with minor variations under a number of marque names. The cabin dimensions of this car were used as a target when Issigonis was drawing up the ADO16.**

Len Lord felt that the new medium-sized car deserved top-quality styling, and bypassed his own styling team to give the job to Pininfarina. By January 1959 this is what the fashionable Italian styling house had designed.

BMC's production engineers and stylists then got to work on the Pininfarina design to make it more suitable for production and to improve its aerodynamics. By July 1959 this design was now in place, carrying the internal designation ADO16. The grille details would be changed before production began three years later.

decided that the car needed a more modern style to give it additional sales appeal. So later that year, Pininfarina was asked to work its magic on the car. Models were shipped across to Italy, and BMC stylist Dick Burzi visited the Pininfarina studios with body engineer Reg Job to explain what BMC wanted. By January 1959 a full-size model of the initial Pininfarina proposal had reached Longbridge. Interestingly, this was a four-door saloon, even though the early prototypes had only two doors.

Although this was on the right lines, its slab front and peaked headlamps were rejected as likely to create too much wind resistance, and the BMC body engineers felt that the shapes of the windscreen and rear window apertures would give trouble in production. So the Pininfarina design was reworked in-house at Cowley, and by July 1959 something very close to the production design had been achieved. The BMC engineers had widened the car by a few inches to allow for a full-width bench rear seat capable of seating three people, and introduced curved side glasses (then very new in the UK motor industry) as part of this widening process. Later, two-door and estate derivatives would be based on the four-door design, and both would be drawn up in the UK, although the final designs were also passed to Pininfarina as a matter of courtesy.

PROTOTYPES

Now that the car was getting close to its production form, it was given a new designation. XC9002 had indicated that it was in the experimental stage; now it became ADO16. The Mini project had been ADO15 – the fifteenth design from the Amalgamated Drawing Office that had united the old Austin and Morris drawing offices – and the later large car, which had once been X9001 and would become the BMC 1800 at its launch in 1964, took the ADO17 name. Despite the dominance of Longbridge within BMC, quite a lot of the detail design work was actually done at the old Morris premises in Cowley, which would of course build a proportion of the cars once they were ready for production.

Once the basic design was in place, ADO16 was handed over to Charles Griffin (BMC's Chief Engineer for Passenger Cars) to take forward to production. Griffin moved from Cowley to Longbridge to do the job, becoming Issigonis's deputy in the process. He also had far more to do with ADO16 than has generally been acknowledged. As he explained to Graham Robson in an interview for *Mini Magazine*, Issigonis was not really interested in the car; he was totally absorbed by work on the Mini. 'He had the other models in his peripheral vision,' said Griffin, 'but no concentration on them at all. He was a genius though, no doubt.' Meanwhile, serious work had also begun on the third model of that original trio of XC cars conceived under Len Lord. Issigonis divided his engineering teams into three 'cells': A-Cell focused on the Mini, B-Cell focused on ADO16, and C-Cell focused on the big car, the ADO17 that eventually became the 1800 'Land Crab'.

The first prototypes of what was recognizably the eventual production ADO16 took to the roads in 1960. Engineering development was based at the old Morris works in Cowley, near Oxford. A dozen cars were built for development work and were tested both on continental European roads and at the MIRA proving ground near Nuneaton in the Midlands. In those days, relatively little care was taken over secrecy and attendant disguise, and there was in any case far less public curiosity about unreleased car designs than has since become the case. So when the October 1960 issue of *Motor Sport* carried a 'scoop' photograph of an ADO16 prototype, the magazine was gentlemanly enough not to suggest it might be a Morris even though it was running on an Oxford trade plate! A French motoring magazine also caught a prototype on test and published a photograph.

A second batch of a dozen 'improved' prototypes was built and tested during 1961, and by the end of the year the car had been signed off for production. The first production examples, wearing Morris badges, were assembled at Cowley in January 1962, although the launch was planned for the Earls Court Motor Show that autumn to give production time to build up so that BMC would be able to meet the expected demand for their new car. This period was also used to refine the design and specification differences between the different models. Most of these would enter production later – Austins in 1963, Rileys and Wolseleys in 1965 – although the MG derivatives were launched alongside the Morris models in 1962. The Vanden Plas derivatives that were introduced in 1963 were nevertheless not envisaged at this stage, and nor were they designed by BMC, as Chapter 6 explains.

The car that entered production in 1962 as the Morris 1100.

BADGE ENGINEERING

The ADO16 was adapted to suit customers for no fewer than six of the old-established marques that had been brought together under the BMC umbrella in 1952. There would eventually be versions with Austin, MG, Morris, Riley, Wolseley and Vanden Plas badges, and outside the UK there would be versions of the car that carried Authi badges (in Spain) and Innocenti badges (in Italy).

Although MG, Riley and Wolseley employees could take no credit for the ADO16 design, it is very noticeable that Austin and Morris people both tended to promote 'their' marque's contribution to the design. The old rivalries died hard.

The **ADO16** range spread during the 1960s, although by the time of this 1971 picture showing the Mk III cars it had been somewhat reduced by British Leyland's attempts at model rationalization.

THE RECKONING

As already noted, ADO16 rapidly became a best-seller in its home market, and it maintained that position for most of its production life. It was assembled not only in the UK but also in a number of overseas locations (see Chapter 7). There were locally manufactured versions abroad, too, as that same chapter explains. So in terms of its acceptance as a product, the car can only be judged as a huge success. At its peak in 1965–6 it was being assembled at a rate of just under 280,000 a year in Britain.

This success inevitably had its impact on the motoring scene in several different ways. For car buyers, the significance of ADO16 was that

It was George Harriman, by then BMC's Managing Director, who settled on a policy of advanced engineering to help give BMC what would now be called a Unique Selling Point.

it changed expectations in the mid-size saloon market. It gave the family owner the benefits of modern technology – front-wheel drive and ruthless packaging efficiency – at an affordable price, and it showed how advanced technology could be employed unobtrusively for the benefit of the consumer. For its makers at BMC, it also advanced the company's strategy – settled by Managing Director George Harriman in 1960 – of aiming for engineering excellence. (In practice, this was done because BMC did not have the resources to change models as frequently as its main rivals, Ford and Vauxhall.) Along with the Mini, it helped to alter worldwide perceptions of BMC, creating an image of a company that led with high technology to replace the old image of a stolid, conventional manufacturer that had been current in the 1950s.

ADO16 also had a longer-term effect on the wider European motor industry. In Italy, for example, Fiat very quickly latched onto the idea of using front-wheel drive for space-saving. All the company's small cars in the 1950s had used a rear-mounted engine with rear-wheel drive, but chief designer Dante Giacosa borrowed the BMC concept and modified it, putting the gearbox end-on and above the differential rather than in the sump, and using unequal-length drive shafts. Fiat were nevertheless unsure about the concept and decided to market the new car under their Autobianchi brand. The Autobianchi Primula was released in 1964, looking more than a little like the ADO16, and in 1965 the car came second in the European Car of the Year awards. In due course, it would be the Fiat engine and transmission layout, rather than the BMC type, that would become the standard for front-wheel-drive cars.

Imitation is the sincerest form of flattery, and the Autobianchi Primula of 1964 actually looked a lot like the ADO16 that had inspired it. Although its engine was mounted transversely and drove the front wheels, it used an end-on gearbox.

Replacements – sort of. The Morris Marina was a deliberately conventional car, aimed at people who had liked the Morris Minor 1000. The Austin Allegro did at least take forward some of the advanced engineering seen in ADO16, but was never much liked. The bigger-engined versions of both were intended to counter sales of the Ford Cortina.

Arguably, then, ADO16 was one of the cars that contributed to the British motor industry's excellent reputation in the 1960s. However, behind the scenes there were undoubtedly problems. BMC was still struggling to get to grips with the large numbers of factories and dealership chains it had inherited, and the need to keep all those factories busy and to produce multiple different 'badge-engineered' versions of the same car made manufacturing costs higher than a more streamlined company like Ford was able to achieve.

These problems had not been ironed out before 1968, when BMC (which had become BMH, British Motor Holdings, in 1966) merged with the Leyland Motor Corporation to form the British Leyland Motor Corporation. That brought several more manufacturers into the corporate fold, with several more factories and several more rival model line-ups. British Leyland never really got to grips with all these – although the results of their early attempts were evident in changes to the ADO16 range in the late 1960s. Sadly, the task of unifying so many different companies was more than they could handle and one of the casualties was the forward-looking engineering that had gone into the BMC cars of the 1960s.

A further problem was that some aspects of the ADO16 design had not been thought through as fully as would be the case today. Alec Issigonis had perhaps been given too much control over the final product, and Graham Turner highlighted an example of this in his seminal book *The Leyland Papers*. Fleet sales accounted for about one-third of domestic car sales in the UK in the 1960s and, despite its widespread acceptance by private motorists, the ADO16 lost out to the Ford Cortina here for one simple reason: its boot was too small for travelling salesmen. As Turner says: 'Alec Issigonis … might humorously describe a large boot as "a sales gimmick" but it was an essential ingredient of the "value for money" formula which the Ford Cortina was designed to embody.' It is at least arguable that the problem was known and understood within British Leyland – after all, a 'booted' version of the car was developed on their watch to become the Austin Apache in overseas markets (*see* Chapter 7).

Despite its undoubted sales success, ADO16 never quite achieved its full potential. Its manufacturer's profits were always minimal; for many years the multiple model variants made the range far more confused than it needed to be; and shortcomings of the design were not rectified as quickly as they should have been. In so many ways, the car stands as a metaphor for the whole of the British motor industry that collapsed after its finest hour in the 1960s.

WHERE WERE THEY BUILT?

The plan to build multiple different versions of the ADO16 to suit all the BMC marques implied production on a scale that the company had never before attempted. A complicated system was drawn up, using the Austin works at Longbridge and the Morris works at Cowley as the final assembly plants for all UK-built variants. (There would of course also be assembly in some overseas plants, using Knocked Down kits supplied from the UK.)

These two plants played a game of Box and Cox in order to achieve the high volumes and the model mix required at any one time. Longbridge was a larger and more modern factory than Cowley, and not surprisingly assembled the lion's share of all ADO16s. Most of its ADO16s were assembled in CAB2 (Car Assembly Building no 2), which was specially built for the purpose during 1962. However, all the estate variants were assembled alongside Minis in the older CAB1 plant, which also saw assembly of small numbers of saloons when demand was high.

Supplies of parts and sub-assemblies were fed into these two end-points not only from other factories within the BMC empire but also from major component suppliers such as Lucas, Smiths Industries and others. The body-in-white was pressed and built at five different locations. These were Austin at Longbridge (in the old West Works), Fisher & Ludlow at Castle Bromwich (who pressed panels for Riley and Wolseley models but also built all the estate bodies), Nuffield Metal Products in Birmingham (which built saloon bodies for Cowley), and Pressed Steel at Cowley and Swindon (which

The sheer scale of the ADO16 production operation demanded the involvement of a number of factories. These are 1100 Mk I body shells on the lines at the Pressed Steel works in Cowley.

supplied both the Cowley and the Longbridge lines). All engines and gearboxes came from Longbridge.

Build locations for the different marques were as follows:

Austin
The Mk I saloons were mainly built at Longbridge, although some were also built at Cowley. All estates and all Mk II and Mk III models were built at Longbridge.

MG
All MG models were built at Cowley.

Morris
The vast majority of Morris models were built at Cowley, although there was some manufacture of saloons at Longbridge as well, and all Morris estates were Longbridge-built.

Riley
The Riley derivatives were initially built at Longbridge, but production transferred to Cowley during the Mk II era and remained there until the end in 1969.

Vanden Plas
Although BMC liked to give the impression that the Vanden Plas derivatives were hand-built at that company's works in Kingsbury, in practice they were not: the Vanden Plas works was far too small to cope with such volumes. So the cars were initially built at Longbridge, subsequently transferring to Cowley from about 1968 with the other low-volume derivatives.

Wolseley
The Wolseley models entered production at Longbridge in 1965, but then moved to Cowley, probably during 1968.

These complicated production arrangements were not cost-effective. As Graham Turner commented in *The Leyland Papers*,

> Pressings for the 1100-1300 range came from Swindon and Llanelli and the body shells were then shipped from Swindon to both Cowley and Long-bridge for painting and trimming: the cost penalty for double assembly, according to the British Leyland planners, was at least £5 per model. Similarly there were wide cost variations between the four plants which produced bodies for the group: it was twice as expensive to make them at the plant at Castle Bromwich in Birmingham, where the Countryman models were assembled, as at Swindon.

THE A-SERIES ENGINE

All engines used in the ADO16 were variants of the BMC A-series, an overhead-valve design that had originally been drawn up as an 803cc type for the Austin A30, which was launched in 1951. Almost as soon as the BMC merger took place in 1952, the A-series was earmarked as the engine that would eventually replace the variety of small 4-cylinder types that BMC had inherited from its constituent marques.

The original 803cc engine was enlarged to 948cc by increasing the bore size, and in this guise entered production in 1956. From 1959 the larger bore was combined with a shorter stroke to deliver the 848cc size needed for the Mini – the first transverse derivative of the engine. There was then another derivative with completely revised bore and stroke dimensions to give the long-stroke 997cc engine of the original Mini Cooper in 1961. Chronologically, the 1098cc engine of the 1100 models was the next new version, entering production in 1962.

BMC reasoned that ADO16 needed a new engine of larger capacity and greater power, and so a 1098cc version was created out of the 948cc type by enlarging both the bore and the stroke.

There was one more step between the 1098cc engine and the start of the line that led to the 1275cc engine used in the later 1300 models. This was the 998cc size, introduced for Minis in 1963 and developed as a short-stroke derivative of the 1098cc size. The next stage saw the bore centres moved to allow a much larger bore of 70.6mm for the 1071cc Mini Cooper S engine; a short-stroke version of this delivered the 970cc 'homologation special' engine that enabled Cooper S models to compete in 1-litre class motor sport events. Then a long-stroke version of this engine (sharing its stroke with the 997cc Mini Cooper engine of 1961) finally delivered the 1275cc engine that was used in the ADO16s from 1967.

HYDROLASTIC SUSPENSION

One of the most interesting technical novelties on the original ADO16 was the Hydrolastic sus-pension, designed around patents taken out by Dr Alex Moulton. BMC retained Moulton as a consultant engineer during the development of the system.

The brand name of Hydrolastic combined the words 'hydraulic' and 'elastic', the former to show that it depended on hydraulic fluid and the latter to suggest flexibility and elasticity. When it was

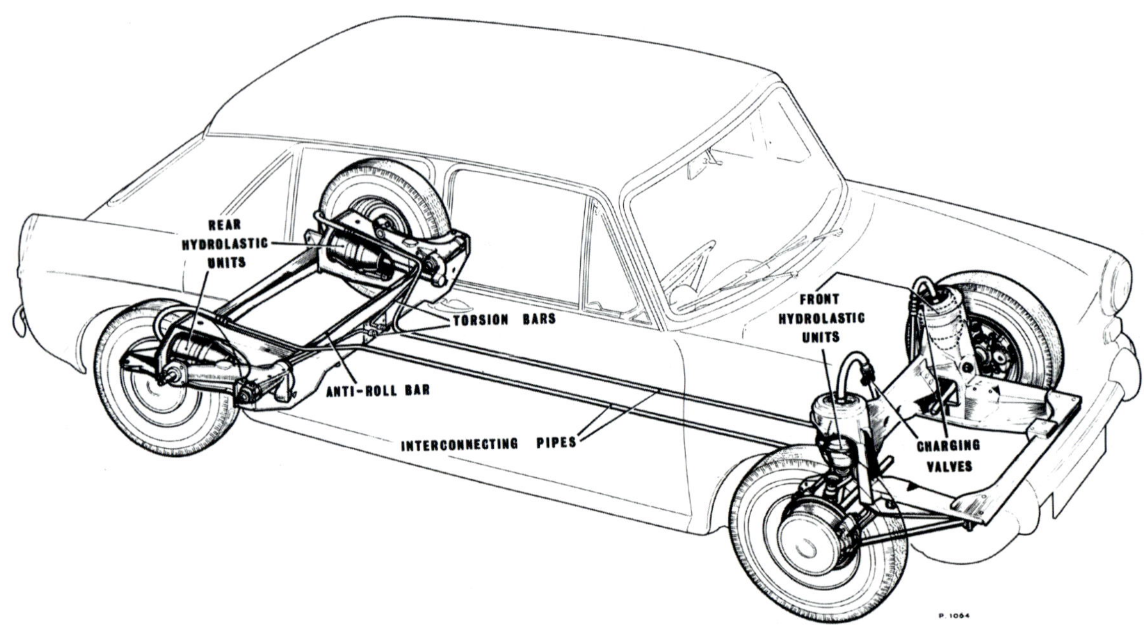

ABOVE: **The transverse engine with its gearbox in the sump had been seen before in the Mini, but the Hydrolastic suspension was new with the 1100. This cutaway drawing was issued to the press in 1962 and showed the layout of the system. There was no cross-linking: each wheel was connected only to the one in front of it or behind it by the hydraulic pipes.**

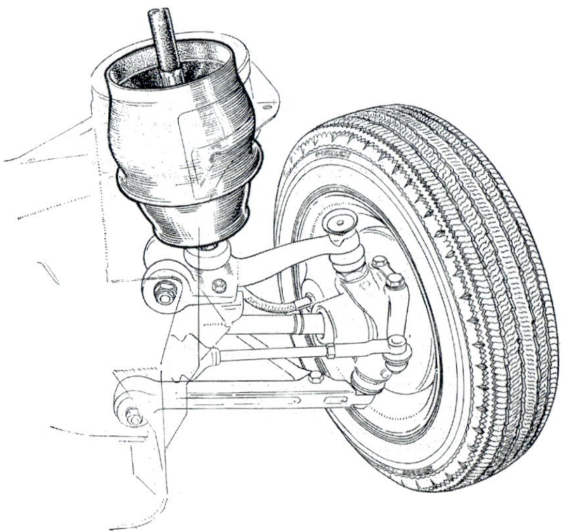

LEFT: **The system was actually manufactured by Dunlop, who proudly appended their name to this picture, which shows the left-hand front wheel suspension of an 1100.**

BMC issued this picture to show how the Hydrolastic system eliminated pitch and 'controlled' bounce; in practice, bounce was sometimes a problem with the Hydrolastic suspension.

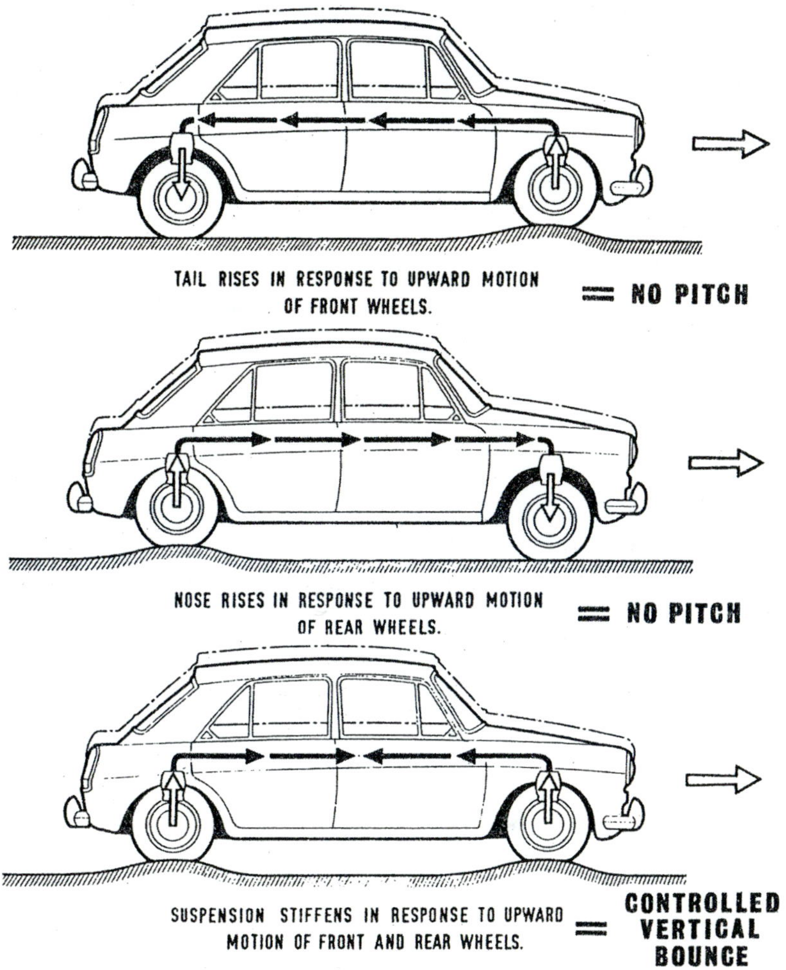

This well-known publicity picture was issued when the MG 1100 was launched in 1962. It shows the Hydolastic suspension in action. Note how the car remains level, even though front and rear wheels are at opposite extremes of their suspension travel.

introduced in 1962 there were many in the motor trade and among the public who mistrusted it (as so often happens with new technology). However, Hydrolastic proved to be a largely problem-free system. It gave a superbly smooth ride without compromising handling.

The car's 'springs' were rubber cones, as on the BMC Mini. Underneath these were chambers that contained the hydraulic fluid, which was a mixture of water and anti-freeze and was kept under high pressure by an engine-driven pump. If the front wheels hit a bump, the fluid was forced through spring-loaded, conical flap valves that acted as dampers, and deflected the rubber springs. Small-bore pipes connected the front and rear suspension units on each side of the car. Fluid forced out of the front chambers by the front wheels hitting a bump travelled through these pipes to the rear units, so forcing the rear wheels downwards to maintain the car on an even keel.

THE SHAPE OF THINGS TO COME

Perhaps keen to win more business from the company, which had by then become BLMC, Italian design house Pininfarina drew up a prototype body style around the running-gear of the BMC 1800 saloon and presented it at the 1967 Motor Show. A year later, it followed up with a similar design based on 1100 running-gear, and this time presented the result at its home motor show in Turin. Pininfarina's choice of an ADO16 for its second concept car was a clear indication of the esteem in which the motor industry generally held the ADO16 design.

The two concept cars, which were quite radical for the time, were both streamlined two-box saloons with greatly improved aerodynamics. Both had a sloping rear window that opened, so prefiguring the 'hatchback' concept. Sadly, however, BLMC was not interested in taking these ideas further. In the real world, broadly similar designs were not far off, and the 1971 Citroën GS incorporated many of the ideas that Pininfarina had showcased in these two cars.

Pininfarina had a second stab at designing bodywork for the ADO16 in 1968, but BLMC (as they were by then) showed no interest in his concept car. Such designs soon became the norm, making the production ADO16 look old-fashioned.

SRV5 RESEARCH CAR

In the early 1970s British Leyland embarked on a series of safety research vehicles, trying out a number of new technologies. The fifth one in the series was SRV5 (Safety Research Vehicle No. 5), which was constructed in 1974 from a two-door 1300. By this stage, ADO16 was at the end of its life, so there was never any realistic possibility that the safety systems would have been incorporated in production models.

The car's nose was modified to improve pedestrian safety in an accident. The low-mounted bumper was designed to scoop the unfortunate victim onto the sloping bonnet, when a U-shaped tube would spring up and prevent him or her falling into the road and being further injured. It worked in theory....

The car was restored some years ago by RPM Workshops in Chesterfield, and now forms part of the collection at the Heritage Motor Centre in Gaydon.

The SRV5 research car was used for research into a method of improving pedestrian safety, and was based on a two-door 1300.

RALLYING 1100s

Believe it or not, BMC did enter two ADO16s as works rally cars in the 1962 Liège-Sofia-Liège event. Both were Morris 1100s and both had experimental twin-carburettor engines. The Liège-Sofia-Liège rally was notoriously hard on cars of all types, and despite the presence of experienced crews (Pat Moss with Pauline Mayman in 677 BRX, and Peter Riley with Tony Cash in 877 BRX), the two cars did not cover themselves with glory.

That was not quite the end of the ADO16's rallying story, though. In 1969 BMC Australia did an endurance run with a locally built Morris 1500 in an attempt to boost poor sales (*see* Chapter 7). The aim was to achieve 15,000 miles in ten days – or 1,500 miles a day in a car called the 1500. That same year, British Leyland entered some two-door 1300s in motorcross events in the UK.

CHAPTER TWO

AUSTIN AND MORRIS: THE CORE MODELS, MK I, 1962–7

Arguably, this chapter would have been more appropriately titled 'Morris and Austin: the Core Models', because it was the Morris version of the new ADO16 that was introduced first. Badged quite simply as a Morris 1100, the new saloon was announced on 15 August 1962, and made its grand entrance at the Earls Court Motor Show, which opened on 17 October. BMC publicity of the time bullishly claimed that the new car was expected to remain in production for at least ten years – a statement designed to suggest that its design and engineering would remain up-to-date for far longer than its rivals could achieve.

Why was the Morris version the first one to be announced? Some commentators have suggested that there was a background of bickering among the dealers representing the various BMC marques, and that the Morris dealers had scored a notable victory by getting the new car into their showrooms before their Austin rivals. The truth is probably rather more prosaic: space became available to install the new production lines at Cowley, traditional home of the Morris marque, before it became available at Austin's Longbridge factory. So the new model naturally became a Morris: at this stage of the game it would have been unthinkable to build an Austin at Cowley, although things would change over the next few years.

Only the four-door version of the car was made available for the UK market, and in De Luxe form (basic versions were really for export) it cost £505 plus £190 7s 9d Purchase Tax, or £695 7s 9d in all without extras. There were plenty of extras to be had, of course, although there was nothing like the variety of options that car buyers expect in the early twenty-first century. The big excitement about choosing a new car in the early 1960s was in deciding what colour to have. Morris offered a choice of six, plus four interior colour options.

By the time the Morris 1100 went on display at Earls Court in September, it had already been joined by the second of the ADO16 models. This was the MG 1100, also built at Cowley (of course) but available only with the two-door body. This distinction made model differentiation that much clearer for UK buyers: the family car had four doors, and Morris were family cars; the sporty model had just two doors, and MGs were sporty cars. Outside the UK, things were a little more complicated.

The Morris stand at Earls Court was number 118, and it featured three 1100 exhibits. All were special in some way, and the closest to the car that UK buyers might actually aspire to own was a left-hand-drive Tartan Red De Luxe model with Dove Grey leather upholstery (an extra), a heater (an extra) and whitewall tyres (an extra). There was a Connaught Green car, too, this time with right-hand drive, Porcelain Green upholstery and the extra-cost options of front seat belts, a heater and whitewall tyres. Bonnet and boot lid were made of Perspex to show onlookers the size of the boot and the transverse engine configuration, which was still a novelty despite the success of the Mini. The third exhibit was a sectioned 1100 in Pale Lilac with White upholstery that was intended to show the 'transversely mounted power unit and the simple layout of the Hydrolastic suspension', according to the show catalogue.

The Morris was the first ADO16 variant to reach the market in October 1962. The new Hydrolastic suspension was marketed with the slogan 'float on fluid'. Note that the car pictured actually has clear lenses for its front indicators, not the amber ones required on UK models.

If these exhibits seemed a little remote from reality, show-goers could get closer to the real thing on other stands. BMC made use of its subsidiaries to ensure that there were several 1100s on view: body manufacturers Pressed Steel on stand 74 had a Smoke Grey four-door with Blue-Grey upholstery, while Fisher & Ludlow had another four-door De Luxe model on stand 80. Although Fisher & Ludlow would certainly supply bodies for the ADO16 range in later years, their involvement at this early stage was distinctly questionable!

The subtleties of badge engineering that were in the BMC corporate plan were not yet relevant to potential buyers. What they saw was a version of the car that had a grille with multiple horizontal bars and the circular Morris 'bull' motif on bonnet and boot lid. On the inside, the front seats adjusted forwards and backwards but not for rake, and the instrument panel was a trapezoid shape set into the facia – modern in appearance, but not at all frightening to a conservatively minded buying public. The speedometer within that instrument panel was semicircular, the background of the facia was unremarkable matt black, and there were open gloveboxes for oddments stowage. The external bonnet release was only to be expected (the luxury of an internal release was confined to more expensive cars) and the fact that a heater cost extra was no surprise at the time, either.

The British motoring press generally was deeply impressed by the new 1100. When *Autocar* reported

Between them, Pininfarina and the BMC stylists had made an excellent job of the ADO16. The lines were clean and elegant, and quite unlike anything else on the road at the time. For a medium-sized family saloon, it was a real breakthrough. This publicity picture shows a 1966 Morris, which looked exactly the same as the 1962 original.

Morris models had a unique and distinctive cowled instrument panel, with open cubbyholes on the dashboard. Quite why the photographer thought the steering wheel would look better at an angle for this publicity shot has never been revealed.

on a Morris 1100 in its issue dated 17 August 1962, it had already tested the car over some 2,000 miles, and it had this to say:

> The staff of this journal have never before been so unanimously enthusiastic about the overall qualities of a car; the few criticisms are minor in character. It is obvious that a farsighted and thorough engineering job has been done – a remark which applies not only to the more obscure technicalities, but to the finish and general layout which will strike most people first. It is fully capable of challenging all the currently popular European small cars which it is destined to meet in world markets. Of greater importance, in our opinion it can out-sell them if supported by equal after-sales service and if the quality inspection at the factory is such that all are assembled faultlessly.

Of great interest was the new Hydrolastic suspension. *Autocar*'s 2,000 miles of experience plus examination of components and discussion with engineers had convinced them 'that the system is well made and simple; in brief, there is no reason to suspect that the suspension system should not prove as reliable as any other more orthodox arrangement'. It worked, too: 'The unanimous view of the test staff is that on overall rating for ride comfort on smooth or rough roads at all speeds, controllability in these conditions, adhesion in the wet or dry, inherent safety and steering response, there is no better car, irrespective of size.'

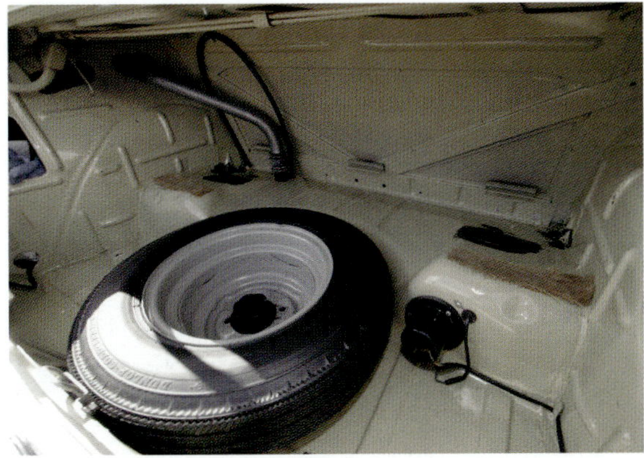

ABOVE: **Although the boot was not enormous, it was big enough for most family requirements. BMC made it as large as possible by putting the spare wheel in a well below the boot floor. The wheel in this shot really is round – the camera angle has distorted it.**

LEFT: **At the time ADO16 was being designed, the influence of American tail fins was all-pervasive. Other Pininfarina designs for BMC had them, so it was only to be expected that ADO16 would, too.**

Everything was neatly packaged under the bonnet. Engines carried a metal plate bearing the Austin or Morris name, as appropriate, but there were no other differences between them. This is a display cutaway – in fact, of a 1966 Austin Countryman.

THE EXTRAS

The May 1963 UK sales brochure for the Morris 1100 offered the following optional extras:

Fresh-air heater/demister or fresh-air system without heater
Laminated windscreen
Leather upholstery
Over-riders (standard on De Luxe models)
Weathermaster tyres
Whitewall tyres

The following accessories were selected from a longer list:

Anti-mist panels	Hand tools
Auxiliary lamps	Roof rack
Badge bar	Seat belts
Car valeting items	Seat covers
Exhaust trim	Touch-up paints
Fire extinguishers	Wing mirrors

Of interest is that car manufacturers offered two reasons for not fitting seat belts as standard at the time. One was that, if fitted during assembly, they would be subject to Purchase Tax, whereas if bought as an accessory, they were not. The other was that not supplying cars with belts gave customers a freedom of choice among different makes that they would otherwise not have had.

THE DE LUXE MODELS

The De Luxe version of the Morris 1100 was more or less standard in the UK, and brought the following extras over the basic specification:

Front door panniers
Opening rear quarter-windows
Passenger's sun visor
Spare wheel
Stainless steel window frames
Temperature gauge

There were minor criticisms, but these went almost unnoticed in the welter of praise heaped on the car. The steering wheel position was not ideal, and some testers felt the pedals were too small. The absence of bottom-gear synchromesh came in for criticism because most rival cars had it. The boot was not large, although it was large enough. On the positive side, the car was fully waterproof (early Minis had not been), the brakes were light and progessive, and 'particularly surprising are the smoothness and tractability of the engine throughout the range'.

Performance was not especially good, though. 'In a car with such good road-holding, some owners will undoubtedly want more performance, but the 1100 will satisfy most', said *Autocar*. The test figures were 22.2 seconds for the 0–60mph standing start, and a maximum of 77.7mph (125km/h). For the time, these figures were entirely acceptable.

THE AUSTIN 1100 (1963)

Austin dealers got their ADO16s just a year later than their Morris counterparts. The ex-factory price of £505 for a De Luxe model was exactly the same as for the contemporary Morris, although a change in Purchase Tax that followed the 1963 Budget had reduced the overall cost by a not insignificant amount to £610 15s 5d.

Not surprisingly, the Austin had the same specification as its Morris counterpart, although it was of course built at the Longbridge plant. All cars for the UK market had four doors, and the De Luxe model was pretty well standard issue. The requirements of badge engineering meant that it was reasonably easy to distinguish Austin from Morris, though, and the most obvious exterior difference was a wavy mesh grille on the Austin, plus of course an Austin shield badge on the bonnet and different hubcaps. Inside, BMC had dared to be a little more adventurous with an ultra-modern strip-type speedometer made by Smiths and similar to that introduced at the same time on the much more expensive new Rover 2000. The similarity can have done no harm to sales of the Austin 1100, although the strip speedometer was a mite too new-fangled for some would-be buyers. They would have gone for the Morris instead – precisely as BMC had intended.

Autocar was certainly not alone in testing the new Austin 1100, but it is interesting to compare some of their comments, published on 18 October 1963, with those they had made a year earlier about the Morris version. The ride and handling were still impressive; the boot space good, but difficult to load. The unsynchronized bottom gear could be difficult to engage with the car at rest, and it was too easy to hit reverse when changing from second to third. The same criticisms of the steering wheel angle and the small pedal pads surfaced. The brakes felt rather dead, but stopped the car well. Performance was adequate: 'While the Austin 1100 may not

This was one of the first publicity pictures of the Austin version. The grille bars and Austin badge in the middle give away its identity in this shot.

The Austin 1100 followed a year after the Morris. Just two features in this picture distinguish it from its Morris stablemate: the 'crinkle-cut' grille bars with an Austin nameplate a third of the way down, and the flying A on the hubcaps.

The Austin dashboard was quite different from the Morris design, with a strip-type speedometer. The two-spoke steering wheel, however, differed only by having the Austin badge at its centre.

The ADO16 design looked good from all angles, which was testament to the good work put in by Pininfarina and the BMC stylists.

be as fast off the mark as some of its immediate rivals, it does move away quite quickly … the best one-way speed reached was 80mph, with a mean of 79mph. On motorways, the Austin 1100 was quite content to cruise all day at about 70mph in reasonable quietness and complete comfort.'

There were some build faults, though. 'On the test car, the joint between the exhaust manifold and pipe failed; this is a fault that has happened on other 1100s and we are surprised that nothing has been done to rectify this weakness.' On the inside, 'until one looks very closely, the interior trimming seems to have been carried out in a very workman-like manner. However, gaps in the facia padding do show welds peeping through.'

The magazine summarized that

in looks, the Austin 1100 is one of the neatest and most handsome small cars on the roads today. While it may lack the punch of some of its rivals, it offers more than most in respect of comfort and quietness. This combined with the exceptional roadholding, makes it an excellent consideration. However, may we repeat the final phrase of the

LEFT: **Austins had this smooth style of boot lid handle; on Morris models, the handle was thicker and fluted.**

BELOW: **This photograph from the Kent Police Museum shows a 1964-registered Austin 1100 with the Police Sergeant who used it. The car is not in Police livery and has an AA badge on the grille that suggests private ownership – although in practice it was used for 'unmarked' duties and carried a Police radio and other equipment.**

Morris 1100 test – 'In our opinion, it can outsell them (foreign rivals) if supported by equal after-sales service, and if the quality inspection at the factory is such that all are assembled faultlessly.'

The clear implication was that *Autocar* doubted BMC would be able to meet all those requirements.

OUTSIDE THE UK

Although British buyers were offered only four-door models with Austin and Morris badges, the two-door body that they could buy only with MG badges was available as an Austin and as a Morris in export markets. Right from the start in August 1962, Denmark had a two-door 1100 that was badged as a Morris Marina. The Netherlands followed in 1963 with a two-door 1100 that was sold as an Austin Glider. That name was probably chosen as a deliberate reference to the 'floating' ride provided by the Hydrolastic suspension.

Details of the 1100 models assembled abroad will be found in Chapter 7.

For the new Morris 1100

Body shell by Pressed Steel Company

PRESSED STEEL COMPANY LIMITED

Makers of Britain's first production all-steel car body in
1926, suppliers to the motor industry ever since.

FACTORIES: COWLEY, OXFORD · THEALE, BERKSHIRE · PAISLEY, SCOTLAND · SWINDON, WILTSHIRE

Head Office: Cowley

Manufacturers also of Prestcold refrigerators and domestic appliances,
railway rolling stock, pressings of all types, and executive aircraft.

ABOVE AND OPPOSITE: **Though Pressed Steel at Cowley was not the only supplier of ADO16 bodies, it made sure to promote its involvement early on. A year after it placed the Morris advertisement, it took out a similar one for the Austin models.**

Pressed Steel Company

are proud to be associated with
the new Austin 1100

PRESSED STEEL COMPANY LIMITED

Makers of Britain's first production all-steel car body in
1926, suppliers to the motor industry ever since.

FACTORIES : COWLEY, OXFORD · THEALE, BERKSHIRE · PAISLEY, SCOTLAND · SWINDON, WILTSHIRE

Head Office: Cowley

Manufacturers also of commercial refrigeration equipment, domestic appliances,
railway rolling stock, pressings of all types, and executive aircraft.

PERFORMANCE CONVERSIONS

Aftermarket tuning specialists were very familiar with the BMC A-series engine and so, even though the 1100's 1098cc version was new, the first performance enhancements were developed during 1962 and were ready by the turn of the year. Speedwell and Downton, both well known at the time, were first into the market, and others followed.

Motor magazine tested a Speedwell-converted Morris 1100 four-door in its issue dated 6 February 1963. 'Depressed by the inbuilt restrictions of the standard A-series cylinder head that is found on all the small BMC cars,' they wrote, 'Speedwell have designed their own special head in light alloy: this is the basis of their 1100GT kit.' Like the MG 1100 version of the engine already available, this depended on twin carburettors, but the Speedwell conversion eclipsed the MG's power output by a huge margin. The MG had 55bhp; the Speedwell conversion, with the company's own Supertone exhaust system, delivered 67bhp at 5,500rpm on twin 1¼-inch SUs or 72bhp at 6,000rpm on twin 1½in SUs.

Speedwell claimed 0–50mph acceleration of approximately 10 seconds with the bigger carburettors, but *Motor* was unable to test that because of weather conditions. Nevertheless, it did record a top speed of 95mph (the standard car peaked at 81.4mph), and much improved acceleration in the gears, together with fuel consumption that was very similar to the standard model's.

The basic kit cost £75, and the larger carburettors £15 extra. Speedwell would also provide a rev counter (£17 10s 0d), Restall front seats with adjustable rake (£16), and an Interior Silent Travel kit (£7 10s 0d).

Autocar tested a Downton conversion four years later in its 23 March 1967 issue. In this case, the conversion was actually fitted to a Morris 1100 Traveller. Downton skimmed the cylinder head to raise the compression ratio to 9.2:1, reworked the combustion chamber design, fitted a single HS4 carburettor and used a Mini Cooper-type two-branch exhaust manifold. The test car gave a maximum speed of 95mph and would reach 60mph from rest in 16.2 seconds. Total cost of the conversion was £92 5s 9d, the original cylinder head being taken in exchange for the modified type.

Downton also made their conversion available for automatic-transmission cars, using a higher 9.6:1 compression ratio. As these cars already had an HS4 carburettor as standard, the conversion cost was actually cheaper by £17 10s 0d.

THE AUTOMATIC MODELS (1965)

Since the mid-1950s BMC been working closely with Automotive Products (AP) of Leamington Spa to develop its own automatic gearbox. Automatic transmissions were already popular in the USA, but the American-built types were not suitable for most UK-built cars because they were designed to operate with the large and lazy engines typical of American cars of the time. Although a few semi-automatic gearboxes did appear in the UK during the 1950s, they were never very popular, and only by the end of the decade did the US-designed Borg Warner three-speed transmission enter production in the UK for larger-engined cars such as Jaguars and Rovers.

BMC and AP wanted to develop a gearbox that would work in the typical UK family car, and their project was given a new slant when BMC focused on its new range of front-wheel-drive cars. The transverse engine layouts in the ADO15 Mini, the ADO16, and the later ADO17 'Land Crab' demanded a much more compact design than was yet available. An early prototype of the new AP gearbox was ready by 1962, when it was

The AP automatic gearbox that became optional in 1965 was a compact unit that fitted into the space otherwise occupied by the four-speed manual gearbox. This cutaway diagram shows key components.

The selector gate for the automatic gearbox had its own plinth, and a long selector lever with a T-handle at the top. Unlike conventional automatics, it had no Park (P) position.

installed experimentally in a Mini and gave excellent results.

Further development focused on a four-speed gearbox rather than the three-speed design tried in the Mini. The objective was to make it work as a fully automatic transmission or as a clutchless four-speed manual that allowed the driver to select gears. The gearbox was also designed to use engine oil rather than conventional automatic transmission fluid – a development that was entirely logical in view of its intended location in the sump of the transversely mounted A-series engine.

BMC's decision to take the new four-speed automatic in large quantities prompted AP to move their Purolator filter division into new premises at Bolton in Lancashire and to use the former Purolator factory at Leamington as the production plant for the new gearbox. The key advantage was that the Leamington factory was relatively close to the main BMC factory at Longbridge. BMC, meanwhile, transformed their premises at King's Norton from a store to the assembly plant for the new gearbox and renamed it the Austin No. 2 factory.

The new four-speed automatic gearbox was announced for Minis and ADO16 models alike at the Earls Court Motor Show in October 1965, and became available with immediate effect. Inside the ADO16s, the standard gear lever was simply replaced by a quadrant mounted on the floor with a simple fore-and-aft shift gate and a long selector handle with a T-grip at the top. Curiously, from a modern perspective at least, there was no P or 'Park' position on that gate; the gear selector was left in the N for Neutral position when the car was not in use.

However, the transformation from 1100 to 1100 Automatic was not quite as simple as it might sound. In fact, a special version of the engine accompanied the automatic gearbox. The torque converter of the automatic gearbox put additional strains on the end of the crankshaft, and so this

PAINT AND TRIM COLOURS – AUSTIN MODELS

1100 Mk I (1962–7)

Body	Interior
Alaskan Blue	Fresco Blue
Arabian Grey	Adam Beige, Fresco Blue or Peony Red
Black	Adam Beige, Fresco Blue, Peony Red or Satin Beige
Connaught Green	Adam Beige or Satin Beige
El Paso Beige	Adam Beige, Peony Red or Satin Beige
Honolulu Blue	Adam Beige or Fresco Blue
Laguna Beige	Adam Beige, Fresco Blue or Peony Red
Maroon B	Satin Beige
Tartan Red	Adam Beige or Satin Beige

Maroon B was so called to distinguish it from the earlier unsatisfactory Maroon (retrospectively called Maroon A) used on Morris models in the late 1940s. Maroon A tended to fade. Most sales brochures simply referred to Maroon, although the name Maroon B was commonly used in service literature.

PAINT AND TRIM COLOURS – MORRIS MODELS

1100 Mk I (1962–7)

Body	Interior
Black	Cherokee Red
Connaught Green	Porcelain Green
Dove Grey	Cherokee Red
Fiesta Yellow	Porcelain Green
Old English White	Cherokee Red
Smoke Grey	Blue-Grey
Tartan Red	Dove Grey
Trafalgar Blue	Blue-Grey

engine had a specially modified crankshaft. There was a special cylinder head (which was also used on MG, Riley and Wolseley engines after 1964), and a larger HS4 carburettor to compensate for power losses through the torque converter. Perhaps most important was that the oilways in the cylinder block differed from the standard type, and were designed to allow the lubricating oil to flow in the opposite direction from standard; needless to say, there was a special oil pump to go with it. Buyers had to pay a premium of more

than £50 for the privilege of not having to change gear themselves.

Motor magazine ran an automatic Austin 1100 as a staff car for a while, and reported on 12,000 miles of use in their issue dated 30 September 1967. The report on the transmission was very positive indeed, even though the car had suffered from minor problems in other areas:

In view of the doubts of the rest of the industry, the suspicion of the trade, and the loss of interest engendered by a slow start to production, we are pleased to be able to report that our example of this outstanding automatic transmission has suffered from no mechanical defect (and does not look like doing so) and has performed its appointed task faultlessly.

The magazine went on to add,

you hardly notice that you are not driving the normal product … at 12,000 miles … the automatic changes are smooth except at certain rather unusual combinations of speed and throttle opening, and the ability to select your own gears easily and quickly is as valuable in some conditions as it is unusual. The only criticism one could reasonably make is that the tendency to creep forward when standing in gear is very strong.

Technical Specifications, Austin and Morris ADO16 saloons

Engine
1100 models
BMC A-series 4-cylinder, with iron block and cylinder head
1098cc (64.58 × 83.72mm)
Overhead valves; chain-driven camshaft
Three-bearing crankshaft
Compression ratio 8.5:1 (7.5:1 available for export)
One SU HS2 carburettor (manual gearbox models) or one SU HS4 carburettor (automatic models)
48bhp at 5,100rpm
60 lb ft at 2,500rpm

Transmission
Four-speed manual gearbox, with no synchromesh on first gear
Gear ratios 3.63:1, 2.17:1, 1.41:1, 1.00:1, reverse 3.63:1
Four-speed AP automatic gearbox optional from October 1965; gear ratios 2.69:1, 1.85:1, 1.46:1, 1,00:1, reverse 2.69.
Front-wheel drive

Axle ratio
4.13:1

Suspension, steering and brakes
All-round independent suspension with Hydrolastic units, interconnected front to rear. Front suspension with wishbones; rear suspension with trailing arms and anti-roll bar
Rack-and-pinion steering with 3.125 turns lock-to-lock
Front disc brakes and rear drum brakes

Dimensions

Overall length	12ft 2.7in (3,726mm)
Overall width	5ft 0.4in (1,529mm)
Overall height	4ft 4.7in (1,338mm)
Wheelbase	7ft 9.5in (2,375mm)
Front track	4ft 3.5in (1,308mm)
Rear track	4ft 2.9in (1,292mm)

Wheels and tyres
12-inch steel disc wheels, with 4-inch rims
5.50 × 12 cross-ply tyres

Unladen weights

1100 Mk I 4-door	1,800lb (817kg) approx.

Performance and fuel

0–60mph	22.2 sec
Maximum	78mph (125.3km/h)
Fuel consumption	33mpg (8.58ltr/100km)

These Austin 1100s are going through final inspection at the end of the assembly lines. The place is Longbridge, the date 1963, and all those visible are left-hand-drive models for export. The one nearest the camera has the clear front indicator lenses required in some territories.

AUSTIN AND MORRIS 1100 MK I IDENTIFICATION NUMBERS

Car numbers ('chassis' or VIN numbers)

A A2S10	Austin 1100 Mk I two-door	
A AS10	Austin 1100 Mk I four-door	
M A2S1	Morris 1100 Mk I two-door	
M G2S1	Morris 1100 Mk I two-door	
M AS1	Morris 1100 Mk I four-door	
M GS1	Morris 1100 Mk I four-door	

These prefix codes may be followed by an L for LHD models. Next comes the serial number, which is followed by an A (Longbridge assembly) or an M (Cowley assembly). A full number might therefore read M GS1 56789 A.

Commission numbers

A 16 2S	Austin Mk I two-door
A 2S	Austin Mk I two-door
AM 2S5	Austin Mk I two-door
A 16S	Austin Mk I four-door
M 16 2S	Morris Mk I two-door
M 16 S	Morris Mk I four-door

These prefix codes are followed by the serial number, which in turn is followed by an A, an L or an M on Mk I models. Both A and L appear to indicate assembly at Longbridge, while the M indicates assembly at Cowley.

Body shell numbers

A2S	Austin Mk I two-door	
AMB	Austin Mk I two-door	from 25101
AS	Austin Mk I four-door	
MCB	Morris Mk I two-door	
M2S	Morris Mk I two-door	
MCA	Morris Mk I four-door	
MS	Morris Mk I four-door	

These prefix codes are followed by the serial number, which in turn is followed by the letter A, L or P. A and L appear to indicate Longbridge build, while P indicates Cowley. A full number might therefore read M2S 12345 P.

Engine codes

10AMW	Austin or Morris Mk I 1100
10AG	Austin or Morris Mk I 1100 for automatic transmission
10AH	Austin or Morris Mk I 1100 with Positive Crankcase Ventilation (from 1965)
10AJ	Austin or Morris Mk I 1100 for automatic transmission

On Mk I models, the engine prefix code is followed by a transmission type code and an H (High compression) or an L (Low compression). The transmission type codes were TA (standard-ratio manual gearbox) and A (automatic gearbox). The final segment of an engine number is then the serial number, so that a full number might read 10AMW-TAH123456.

AUSTIN AND MORRIS 1100 PRODUCTION

Production figures were recorded by calendar year, and it is not possible to divide the 1967 figures to separate Mk I from Mk II production. The totals for all Austin and Morris variants – Mk I, Mk II and Mk III – are shown in the next chapter.

CHAPTER THREE

AUSTIN AND MORRIS: THE CORE MODELS, MK II, 1967–71, and MK III, 1971–4

The autumn of 1967 saw a major new-product offensive from BLMC, as Mk II versions of the Mini were introduced alongside Mk II versions of the Austin and Morris ADO16s. The Mk II models were distinguished by a facelift and the range was broadened by the addition of an alternative engine, so that there were now 1300 models as well as 1100 types. The only other mechanical change was to Lockheed swinging-caliper front disc brakes on all models.

The new 1300 models had the 58bhp 1275cc engine that had been tried in some of the more up-market ADO16 models over the summer of 1967 to judge customer acceptance.

Both two-door and four-door saloon bodies remained in production, and the two-doors were now available on the UK market as well as overseas. There were two trim levels for each, De Luxe being the entry-level trim and Super De Luxe being the better-equipped and more expensive version. The arrival of the two-door models allowed BLMC to lower the entry price slightly: at the 1967 Earls Court Motor Show, a two-door Austin 1100 Mk II De Luxe was listed at £647 0s 8d (£525 before Purchase Tax), whereas the entry-level four-door De Luxe models at the same show in 1966 had been priced at £655 12s 9d (£532 before Purchase Tax).

The facelift was hardly a major one, and its most obvious feature was that the rear fins – fashionable when the ADO16s were new – had been cut back. New tail lights were added to suit. At the front, there was a new and wider grille, with six equally spaced horizontal bars on Austins and three groups of three horizontal bars on Morris derivatives. Both cars had a circular marque badge in the centre of this grille, although of course the actual badge differed between them, and the marque name was carried above it. The grille designs of the new 1300s differed from those of the 1100s, to aid recognition. Less immediately obvious was that the front bumper had been raised slightly. All models now had new perforated-disc wheels finished in silver (which sales brochures called 'aluminium') rather than white, and there were side repeater turn signal lamps on the front wings.

Two-door De Luxe models had fixed side windows at the rear, but on Super De Luxe models these windows opened on hinges. The central cowl over the number plate lights on the rear bumper had gone, to be replaced by two separate lights, and the De Luxe models had a simple push-button boot lid release; the long horizontal handle was now reserved for the Super De Luxe models. The De Luxe models had also lost their stainless steel door window surrounds and over-riders, although Super De Luxe models had both. All four-door models had nevertheless lost the stainless steel fillet from the trailing edge of each rear quarter-light. Boot lids all carried new plate-type badges, with the marque name standing out against a black background; script was used for Austin versions and block letters for Morris types, in the traditional way. If the car was an 1100, that number was included on the black background, but if it was a 1300, the number was surrounded by a grey field to aid differentiation.

ABOVE LEFT: **This Austin 1300 Mk II four-door shows the key recognition features of the Mk II models. Note the new grille, the side repeater indicators and the perforated wheel discs.**

ABOVE RIGHT: **By the mid-1960s, tail fins were no longer in fashion, and so the ADO16's fins were pared back for the Mk II models, and the tail lights were redesigned to suit.**

The interior had come in for a facelift, too, and Austin and Morris models now shared a common trim style. The headlining was now a suspended type with its own frame, and was no longer glued directly to the underside of the roof. Upholstery was now in vacuum-formed expanded vinyl, and the side panels and door trims were covered in matching diamond-pattern quilted material. Reclining front seats were optional on the Super De Luxe, which had a new style of upholstery – still in vinyl, of course – while two-door versions shared their front seats with the De Luxe models. The two-door models had a new style of flush release handle on their doors.

De Luxe models came with a new rectangular housing in the centre of the dash, with a simulated wood-grain front panel around a circular speedometer containing a fuel gauge. Rocker switches for lights and wipers flanked the bottom of the dial, while the ignition lock was located at top left and a plunger for the screen washers at top right. There was an open parcels shelf on either side, and the arrangement was common to both LHD and RHD models.

The Super De Luxe models, however, had a dashboard that was more similar to the original 1100 style. This had the still-fashionable strip-type speedometer, with a matt silver facia on Austin models and a crackle-black facia on their Morris

equivalents. Lights and wipers were operated by large rocker-type switches, and there were now green tell-tales for the indicators at the ends of the instrument panel; the column stalk no longer had a light at its tip. All models could now be had with a heated rear window at extra cost.

Gearboxes were either manual or automatic on all models, the first year's production of 1100 manual Mk IIs having the old gearbox with no synchromesh on first gear. An all-synchromesh gearbox had been announced for the 1300 models at their launch, but did not become standard on the 1100s until a year later in September 1968. From the start of Mk II production, the front brakes on 1100 automatics and all 1300s had new single-caliper discs.

Meanwhile, the UK range had been simplified, as it became clearer what customers were buying. The two-door Super De Luxe and four-door De Luxe models in the middle of the range disappeared from the catalogues in spring 1968 (although they remained available in some export markets), leaving just two-door De Luxe and four-door Super De Luxe types still available.

Motor was favourably impressed when it tried a two-door 1300 Super De Luxe in its 2 November 1968 issue. 'The higher gearing combined with the more powerful engine … has made the car much more refined: easy, unfussy cruising at 70mph is now possible. Even the characteristic transfer gear whine has been successfully muted.' Generally, 'performance has been raised to a level which should please both the enthusiast driving one-up and the family man climbing hills with a full load. Yet economy remains almost as good as for the smaller engined car.' (The actual fuel consumption figure was 28.5mpg [9.93ltr/100km] overall, as compared to 31.4mpg [9.01ltr/100km] for the 1100.)

The seats were more comfortable than before, and *Motor* wrote of the 'transformation of the interior: gone are the jumble of ill-assorted colours, dirt-sensitive fabrics, and carpets that looked like flypaper sprayed with horsehair.' The new jacking arrangement was sensible, but the windscreen wipers still left a large area unwiped on the driver's side. The competition had moved on, too. 'Few saloons of any size or price could match the original 1100 for roadholding or cornering power. Now, six years after its introduction, there are several to rival it fairly closely so the superiority has become marginal rather than crushing.'

This Mk II was pictured in enthusiast ownership at a classic car event over the summer of 2014. The car is an 1100, with the simpler grille design used on the smaller-engined cars.

ABOVE LEFT AND RIGHT: **Austin and Morris models were again distinguishable only by badges – and by their hubcaps. The marque name was carried at the top of the grille, and the wheel discs were finished in aluminium, not white as here.**

LEFT: **Tail badges were completely new, and incorporated the Mk II name.**

The engine also carried its own badge, an aluminium plate riveted in the usual place on top of the rocker cover.

The vacuum-formed plastic upholstery of the Mk III cars was not a change for the better. It tended to make the cars feel cheaper, an impression not helped by the wood-grain finish, which looked so false that it was mere tokenism.

Inevitably, perhaps, small details let the car down: 'There remains room for improvement in certain minor ways: no face-level ventilation is provided yet; the sub-frame mountings could perhaps be tuned to give better suppression of road noise, and quality control should not allow those small blemishes and glue stains on the trim.'

THE MK II OUTSIDE THE UK

Denmark continued to go its own way with BLMC products, and followed on from the Morris Marina (its name for the 1100 Mk I) with the Morris Marina GT, which was actually just a Morris 1300 Mk II.

In this period, ADO16s were taken on as Police Panda cars, sometimes replacing the Morris Minors traditionally associated with the role. This 1100 belonged to the West Midlands Police.

CRAYFORD CONVERTIBLES

Bodywork conversion specialists Crayford had developed their own estate conversion of the ADO16 by 1965 (*see Chapter 4*), although the market for this was limited when BMC introduced its own estate just over a year later.

Undaunted, Crayford developed a cabriolet from the two-door 1300 Mk II and sold it through the Caffyn's dealership in Kent, which happened to have a branch next door to the Crayford factory in Westerham. The car was introduced in 1969 but, according to *The Crayford Story* by Crayford co-founder David McMullan, only twelve were sold. The price was from £1,519. Although full details of the cars are not available, pictures of both Morris and MG versions exist.

The Crayford cabriolet was, of course, based on the two-door car. This example is a Morris.

This remained available until 1971, when Denmark began to take the later and better-known car that wore Morris Marina badges. Austin versions of the Mk II ADO16 nevertheless remained available.

Further information about the ADO16 models and derivatives that were assembled abroad may be found in Chapter 7.

AUSTIN AMERICA, 1968–71

Sales of the special MG 1100 Sport Sedan in North America had never been spectacular, although the car had attracted a coterie of buyers. As Chapter 4 explains, the model was withdrawn in the autumn of 1967 as production of Mk I cars came to an end, and another special new model was developed to take its place. Production of this was somewhat delayed and Austin 1100s were used to fill the gap in the USA until the new Austin America was ready.

This new model of course used the Mk II body shell and, as it was a replacement for the two-door MG, it had the two-door version of that shell. Fundamentally, the car was a version of the Austin 1300 Mk II, with an emissions-controlled ('de-toxed') engine and the AP four-speed automatic gearbox as standard, although the all-synchromesh manual gearbox was available as an option. To cope with the range of geographic conditions in the USA, a larger-capacity radiator was also fitted.

The Austin America had a special version of the Austin grille that carried the Austin America name at the top; there was an Austin America plate badge on the boot lid; and there were unique side strips with the Austin America name on the front wing sections. There were special full-size wheel trims, and the first cars had a circular turn signal repeater lamp on each front wing. A driver's door mirror was standard, and so were overriders and a prop for the boot board. These cars also came in a range of colours that included several never made available on any other version of the ADO16.

The Austin-style strip speedometer was fitted, along with additional safety padding and some different switches and controls; these included rocker-type dashboard switches, flush 'letter box' interior door handles, flexible window winder grips and even a padded T-grip for the automatic gearbox selector. There was also a special dished steering wheel with imitation wood rim, two perforated alloy spokes and a collapsible boss. These cars came with special seats, covered in black vinyl with an eight-pleat centre section. The front seats, which of course tipped forwards to give access to the rear, had special catches so that they could not tip forwards in a collision; fixed backrests were standard, but recliners were available as an option. Safety belts were standard both front and rear, those for the rear seats being lap belts only although the cars actually had the mountings for three-point belts.

The Austin America had a number of other special features to meet US emissions and safety requirements. The engine came with exhaust port air injection, a system manufactured by Lucas that used a pump to deliver filtered air at approximately 5psi to a position just behind the valves; here, the surplus oxygen completed burning of any unfired mixture before it passed through the exhaust system. Air was also bled off into the inlet valve ports via a gulp valve to correct an over-rich mixture on the over-run. The petrol tank also had a fuel vapour control system.

Like the MGs sold in the USA, the car came with a laminated windscreen as standard. A heated rear window was standard, too. A hazard warning lights system was fitted, and the brakes had a dual hydraulic circuit with a front-to-rear split and twin master cylinders, and a pressure warning light with its own

The Austin America was a two-door 1300, specially equipped for the USA, where safety and emission regulations were having a major effect on car design. Note the side trim strips on this car, the round marker light ahead of the wheel arch, the wheel embellishers and the large Austin America badge on the grille.

test switch. Wider Dunlop C41 tyres were also fitted, with a 5.95 × 12 size and a six-ply carcass.

This was only the beginning, though. US legislation was changing on an annual basis in this period, and for 1970 more changes had to be made. Side marker lights were mounted below the trim strip on each side, and the strip itself was modified to incorporate a turn signal repeater at each end. Front-seat head restraints were added as standard, and the front seats were fitted on rails to allow them to slide forwards as a way of providing better access to the rear. These later cars also had a British Leyland badge on their left-hand front wings, and the same black vinyl roof and bright roof guttering that were otherwise found only on the 1300GT models. Rubber-faced over-riders were also introduced. For 1971, the range of paint colours changed and the universally black upholstery gave way to a choice of two colours. During this year – really a little late in the car's life – an engine splash-guard became available as a retro-fit.

The car was something of a hit, too. Although not every example was sold in the USA – some were sold in Canada and some in Switzerland – a total of around 58,500 were built between the start of production in March 1968 and its demise in September 1971 as production of the Mk II models generally came to an end. Its replacement was a Federalized version of the Morris Marina, which for North America carried the Austin Marina name.

This neat two-spoke wheel was designed for safety rather than looks. As the picture makes clear, the Austin America had a matt black dashboard with different switches from the mainstream 1300. It also came as standard with the automatic transmission and two-pedal control seen here.

The Austin America had a single-carburettor 1275cc engine, distinguished by the use of an air pump to reduce exhaust emissions. Some of the extra pipework associated with the air injection system is visible in this picture.

VIEWS OF THE AUSTIN AMERICA

When *Road Test* magazine evaluated an early Austin America in its November 1968 issue, the car was priced at $1,985. It was, the magazine reported, 'the first really new British model which could offer a challenge to VW', and early customer response had been very promising: 'At the time of writing, BMH is unable to keep pace with demand for the Austin America.' (BMH, or British Motor Holdings, was the short-lived name for what later became British Leyland.)

'Stylish it is not', but the car was 'forgiving and responsive' and the handling prompted the comment that the car 'feels like an underpowered Mini Cooper S'. The automatic transmission earned praise even though 'using the manual operation, shifts are rather positive'. They were also 'accompanied by momentary revving but are certainly not annoying'.

There were drawbacks, though. The carpets were not fixed and were prone to moving around on the floor (and in July 1971 *Popular Imported Cars* reported that the driver's carpet had worn very badly in the heel area after just 4,000 miles). The ashtray was poorly located – just where the ignition keys would dangle in it – and difficult to remove for cleaning. As for the jack, it was 'antiquated' and 'a device that was obsolete when it was invented'.

THE 1300GT, 1969–74

The overhaul of British Leyland's products continued apace. At the Earls Court Motor Show in October 1969 the new 1300GT models were shown alongside the revamped Mini range. They came with either Austin or Morris badges, and were announced to the public on 1 October, a fortnight before the Motor Show actually opened. This allowed word to get round and dealers to get stock in their showrooms before the Motor Show provided its anticipated boost to sales. Although these were members of the Mk II range, they were not badged as such because there had been no 'Mk I' version before them.

The new 1300GT, which came with a range of new and eye-catching colours, was British Leyland's attempt to inject some excitement into the ADO16 range. It was also a replacement for the Riley Kestrel, which had gone out of production in July. While the MG 1300 models remained available as the traditional sporty variants of the range, the new 1300GTs were carefully priced below them. At Earls Court in 1969, both Austin and Morris cost £909 13s 1d (£695 before Purchase Tax), while the MG was listed at £930 10s 10d (£711 before Purchase Tax).

The pricing strategy was interesting: the MG was resolutely a two-door model while the new 1300GT came with four doors. It offered no performance advantage, and even had the same 70bhp twin-carburettor engine as the MG. What it did offer, though, was a more contemporary image. Ford, Rootes and Vauxhall had all brought out versions of their mid-sized saloons with GT badges and a sporty image, and these had made the British Leyland offerings look rather dowdy. The 1300GT was designed to restore the balance. It was marketed with the slogan of 'the sports saloon that remembers you've got a family'.

All the development effort had gone into making the cars more overtly sporty. The close-ratio gearbox of the MG and Riley 1300 models aided acceleration. Handling had been improved, though very slightly, by lowering the ride height by 0.62in (15.7mm); this in turn was done by reducing the pressure in the Hydrolastic suspension to 205psi from the standard 225psi. There had also been some modifications to the rear suspension, where auxiliary coil springs were now fitted in parallel with the Hydrolastic units, and an anti-roll bar had been added. Between them, these two changes were intended to reduce the car's tendency to switch suddenly from understeer to

The 1300GT picked up some design features from the Austin America. The grille was new, though, and so were the spoked wheel trims. The side trim strip was clearly from the same line of thinking as the America (although the GT was a four-door car and the America a two-door model). Note the British Leyland emblem on the front wing, just behind the wheel arch. This car is a Morris version.

The 1300GT's dashboard had the three-dial design from the now-defunct Riley 1300, but with a black background instead of a wood-grain finish. The three-spoke wheel added an appropriately sporting touch.

Mk III versions of the 1300GT had the latest version of the grille, with three bars to indicate the 1300 engine. As on other Mk III models, there are no longer any side repeater indicators.

oversteer if the accelerator was released in mid-corner.

Appearance counted for most of the 1300GT's character, though: there were new black wheel covers with a 'spoked' design, a fashionable black vinyl roof to accompany several new and somewhat loud colour options, a blacked-out grille, and a thick black metal strip on each flank. Just three colours were available for the first year of production, and all of them were new with the GT: Bronze Yellow, Flame Red and Glacier White were all calculated to look good with the sporty black trim. Both Austin and Morris models had the same '1300GT' badge on the boot lid, while red and silver GT badges added finishing touches on the grille and on each rear window pillar.

The relentless use of black continued inside the car. The seats, with recliners at the front as standard, were upholstered in black vinyl, and so was the dashboard, although its basic three-dial layout with

The 1300GT even had its own special badges on the boot lid and rear quarter-pillars.

a rev counter was carried over from the wooden dash of the Riley Kestrel. The steering wheel, with unique perforated metal spokes, had a black simulated-leather rim, and there was a new and larger interior mirror – with a black body, of course. The gearshift grip was wooden with a black top, and even the sun visors were black. They contrasted with the white vinyl headlining, which had black dots on it to give the impression of a sporty perforated fabric.

Twin windtone horns, two-speed wipers, a big-bore silencer and a reversing light were all included in the standard equipment. The latter was neatly incorporated in the back of the housing for the number-plate light. Optional items included a brake servo, a heated rear window, a laminated windscreen and a steering lock.

The cars also came with 'a new form of jack with a channel section support piece designed to engage with the longitudinal flange under the body sill', as *Motor* reported in its issue dated 4 October 1969. 'The advantages of the arrangement are that the jack can be used at any point along the side to raise either one end of the car only or the whole side, and that there is no need to search for mud-covered engagement points.'

Autocar tested an Austin 1300GT in its issue of 23 October 1969, and was not entirely enthusiastic: 'It is in one or two aspects of comfort and convenience that the 1300GT tends to fall down. On the other hand, the car offers very fair performance, liveliness and excellent handling in a roomy four-door package, at a very reasonable price.'

A good point was the optional brake servo on the test car that 'greatly reduced the pedal pressures needed by comparison with previous 1300s. It also seemed to give the brake pedal a better "feel", with none of the sponginess which formerly characterised the system.' However, the new dashboard came in for criticism: 'The three matching instrument dials are placed so low that not even the tallest driver can see the fuel gauge without craning forward to look over the steering wheel. The critical parts of the speedometer and rev counter scales are similarly obscured.'

Another failing was that there was 'a great deal of mechanical noise at higher speeds ... the other major annoyance is the rather frequent crashing and banging from the area of the rear suspension when the car is driven fast over poor roads.' In fact, that new rear suspension was far from being a success: 'There now seems to be a good deal more harshness over rough surfaces, and both single humps and continuous undulations can produce quite violent bouncing movements which take a long time to damp themselves out. On some minor roads the effect is bad enough to limit cruising speed to 50 or 60mph.'

The yellows and ochre colours so popular on the 1300GT at the time dated very quickly, but the Flame Red of this Mk III 1300GT sets the car's lines off very well indeed. Note that the wheels on this car are a contemporary Dunlop type, and not the originals.

Mk III seats with their redesigned pleating are seen here in a 1300GT – where black went well with the Flame Red exterior.

The Mk II 1300GT models were available for just two seasons, being replaced by Mk III variants in September 1971. From September 1970 the colour range was expanded and a wider choice of interior colours also became available. The Morris range was slightly more restricted than the Austin range, reflecting the lower production capacity at the Morris plant in Cowley. At the same time, and like the other ADO16s, the GT versions gained a steering column lock as standard.

It is worth comparing the dashboard of this Mk III 1300GT with the earlier Mk II type. Note the new air vents at each end.

Bill Boddy tried a Mk III Austin 1300GT for the February 1972 issue of *Motor Sport*, and the notoriously straight-talking veteran journalist was, perhaps surprisingly, rather impressed. 'The BL small cars are as different from Escorts as Brands Hatch is from Spa,' he wrote:

> It is perhaps a good thing that the car-buying public has such diverse views on what it wants. After some very pleasant driving in this Austin 1300 Mk III so-called Gran Turismo saloon I can well understand why this range of little cars, so safe and individualistic, have sold over a million and remain Britain's second best-sellers, sandwiched between Ford's Cortinas and Escorts.

The test car had an unfortunate habit of stalling, which Boddy put down to poor tuning of the twin carburettors. He liked the smaller steering wheel of the GT but complained about the way its spokes obscured the instruments and was not content with the ventilation provided by the latest face-level vents. The cardboard splash-guard nevertheless caught the full weight of Boddy's venom: 'a very poor piece of nineteen-seventies' engineering! That it has only just been deemed necessary, although the basic version of the car was introduced a decade ago, is as remarkable as the precaution is abhorrent.'

MK III MODELS, 1971–4

The final iteration of the ADO16 saloons was prepared for autumn 1971 release. Both 1100 and 1300 engines remained available and the primary focus was on a facelift. In the UK there were no Morris-badged cars, because their place in the British Leyland showrooms was taken from September 1971 by the smaller-engined versions of the new Morris Marina; nevertheless, Mk III Morris saloons did continue in production at Longbridge for those export territories where the Morris name had more resonance than the Austin one. By contrast, Traveller versions of the Morris could still be had in Mk III guise in the UK, because their place had not yet been taken by estate versions of the Marina.

The most obvious element of the Mk III facelift was a new matt-black grille, with a single bright horizontal bar on 1100 Deluxe models and a group of three bars on the 1100 Super Deluxe and the 1300s. There were new badges at the rear, of course, now reading 'Mk III', and a new feature was a British Leyland 'flying wheel' logo just behind the left-hand front wheel arch – but only on the left-hand side, as it was policy right across the British Leyland marques not to have one on the other side. Nobody has yet explained satisfactorily why this was so, although cost-cutting might well have been the reason.

The two-door 1100 version of the Mk III is seen in this publicity picture from when the cars were new. The car is an Austin, as the grille reveals, and it is the single bar on the grille that also reveals that the car is an 1100.

Cost-cutting was certainly on the agenda at British Leyland, and the Mk III models came without bumper over-riders. Inside the passenger cabin, the seats had been restyled yet again, although they still depended on vacuum-formed vinyl for their upholstery. All models had another new facia with circular instruments, and there was a new pear-shaped grip for the gear lever, while the Super De Luxe models also had a smaller-diameter steering wheel with its two spokes in a fashionably moulded shallow triangle shape. On the 1300GT, the oil pressure gauge gave way to an oil pressure warning light. Probably the most useful changes were that two-door models now had anti-burst door locks and that the engine was now protected at the front by a cardboard waterproofing shield. Prices in the UK ranged from £805.63 (£643 before Purchase Tax) for a two-door 1100 to £1,034.38 (£826 before Purchase Tax) for a 1300GT.

Even though the ADO16 range was now nine years old, *Autocar* still found it worthwhile to test one of the Mk III models. Its 14 October 1971 issue carried

Inside a Mk III car, the new two-spoke wheel is apparent, along with the wood-grain dashboard, two-dial instrument set and new air vents.

There were new badges to designate the Mk III models. The 1100 still had a horizontal trim strip on the boot lid; the 1300 did not.

A change for the better! Although it came many years too late, the addition of a splash guard to protect the front-mounted distributor and the plug leads was very welcome on the Mk IIIs. Even that, though, was as cheap as it could be: it was made of cardboard.

an evaluation of a two-door 1300, which concluded that 'it is not difficult to see why the 1100/1300 range is at the top of the British sales charts. Despite its shortcomings in ventilation, it is still a very pleasant, fast and safe car to drive'. What a pity, though, that this late example of the car was exhibiting signs of the poor quality control that was already beginning to afflict cars from British Leyland. On the test car, the steering 'had a tendency to stick rather badly on half left lock'. That this potentially dangerous fault was let out on a press demonstrator car is a sad reflection of the way things were going.

PAINT AND TRIM COLOURS – AUSTIN MODELS

1100 Mk II (1967–71)
1300 Mk II (1967–71)

1968–9 model-years

Body	Interior
Alaskan Blue	Fresco Blue
Aquamarine	Satin Beige
Black	Peony Red
Connaught Green	Satin Beige (Black on early De Luxe and two-door Super De Luxe models)
El Paso Beige	Peony Red
Snowberry White	Black
Tartan Red	Black

1970–71 model-years

Body	Interior
Antelope	Autumn Leaf or Black
Bermuda Blue	Black
Blue Royale	Galleon Blue
Connaught Green	Autumn Leaf
Cumulus Grey	Galleon Blue
Fawn Brown	Autumn Leaf
Flame Red	Black
Glacier White	Black or Icon Red

Austin America (1969–70 model-years)

Body	Interior
Albatross Beige	Black
Antelope	Black
Bermuda Blue	Black
British Racing Green	Black
Bronze Yellow	Black
Chartreuse Yellow	Black
Damask Red	Black
Fawn Brown	Black
Florida Green	Black
Glacier White	Black
Pale Primrose	Black
Peony Red	Black
Riviera Blue	Black
Sable	Black
Snowberry White	Black

Austin America (1971 model-year)

Body	Interior
Bedouin	Autumn Leaf
Blaze	Navy
Bronze Yellow	Navy
Glacier White	Navy
Limeflower	Navy
Racing Green	Autumn Leaf
Teal Blue	Autumn Leaf
Wild Moss	Autumn Leaf

1300GT (1970 model-year)

Body	Interior
Bronze Yellow	Black
Flame Red	Black
Glacier White	Black

1300GT (1971 model-year and Mk III)

Body	Interior
Aqua	Navy
Black Tulip	Geranium
Blaze	Navy
Bronze Yellow	Black or Navy
Flame Red	Black, Geranium or Navy
Glacier White	Autumn Leaf, Black, Geranium or Navy
Green Mallard	Limeflower
Harvest Gold	Olive
Limeflower	Limeflower or Navy
Teal Blue	Autumn Leaf or Teal Blue

1100 Mk III (1971–4)
1300 Mk III (1971–4)

Body	Interior
Aqua	Navy
Black Tulip	Geranium
Blaze	Navy
Bronze Yellow	Navy
Flame Red	Navy
Glacier White	Autumn Leaf or Navy
Green Mallard	Limeflower
Harvest Gold	Olive
Limeflower	Limeflower
Midnight Blue	Geranium or Navy
Teal Blue	Limeflower

PAINT AND TRIM COLOURS – MORRIS MODELS

1100 Mk II (1967–71)
1300 Mk II (1967–71)
1968–9 model-years

Body	*Interior*
Black	Cherokee Red
Connaught Green	Porcelain Green (Black on early De Luxe and two-door Super De Luxe models)
Sandy Beige	Cherokee Red
Smoke Grey	Blue-Grey
Snowberry White	Black
Tartan Red	Cherokee Red (Black on early De Luxe and two-door Super De Luxe models)
Trafalgar Blue	Blue-Grey

1970–71 model-years

Body	*Interior*
Antelope	Autumn Leaf or Black
Aqua	Navy
Bedouin	Autumn Leaf
Bermuda Blue	Black
Blue Royale	Galleon Blue
Connaught Green	Autumn Leaf
Cumulus Grey	Galleon Blue
Fawn Brown	Autumn Leaf
Flame Red	Black or Navy
Glacier White	Black, Geranium, Icon Red or Navy
Limeflower	Limeflower or Navy
Midnight Blue	Geranium or Navy
Racing Green	Limeflower
Teal Blue	Limeflower

1300GT (1969–74)

Body	*Interior*
Blaze	Navy
Bronze Yellow	Black or Navy
Flame Red	Black or Geranium
Glacier White	Black, Geranium or Navy
Limeflower	Navy
Teal Blue	Autumn Leaf

1100 Mk III (1971–4)
1300 Mk III (1971–4)

Body	*Interior*
Antelope	Autumn Leaf or Black
Aqua	Navy
Bedouin	Autumn Leaf
Bermuda Blue	Black
Blue Royale	Galleon Blue
Connaught Green	Autumn Leaf
Cumulus Grey	Galleon Blue
Fawn Brown	Autumn Leaf
Flame Red	Black or Navy
Glacier White	Black, Geranium, Icon Red or Navy
Limeflower	Limeflower or Navy
Midnight Blue	Geranium or Navy
Racing Green	Limeflower
Teal Blue	Limeflower

There were still a few more production changes to come. From April 1973 all cars took on a rod-type gear change borrowed from the Mini and, as this entailed the loss of the original remote gear change casting, a pair of engine steady bars were fixed to the front sub-frame as compensation. A couple of months later, June brought CV joints in place of the original rubber drive couplings.

So the ADO16 saloons reached the end of their production life, available in Britain as De Luxe, Super De Luxe and 1300GT models. In autumn 1973 the new Austin Allegro was announced as their replacement, though the cars remained on sale until the summer of 1974. The very last example was built, without fanfare, in June that year.

Technical Specifications, Austin and Morris Mk II ADO16 saloons

Engine
1100 models
BMC A-series 4-cylinder, with iron block and cylinder
head
1098cc (64.58 × 83.72mm)
Overhead valves; chain-driven camshaft
Three-bearing crankshaft
Compression ratio 8.5:1 (7.5:1 available for export)
One SU HS2 carburettor (manual gearbox models) or
one SU HS4 carburettor (automatic models)
48bhp at 5,100rpm
60 lb ft at 2,500rpm

1300 models
BMC A-series 4-cylinder, with iron block and cylinder
head
1275cc (70.6 × 81.28mm)
Overhead valves; chain-driven camshaft
Three-bearing crankshaft
Compression ratio 8.8:1
One SU HS4 carburettor
58bhp at 5,250rpm
69 lb ft at 3,000rpm
(Lucas air injection fitted on Austin America engines)

1300GT models
BMC A-series 4-cylinder, with iron block and cylinder
head
1275cc (70.6 × 81.28mm)
Overhead valves; chain-driven camshaft
Three-bearing crankshaft
Compression ratio 9.75:1
Two SU HS2 carburettors
70bhp at 6,000rpm
74 lb ft at 3,250rpm

Transmission
Four-speed manual gearbox, with no synchromesh on
first gear with synchromesh on all forward gears from
mid-1968
Gear ratios (1100)   3.63:1, 2.17:1, 1.41:1, 1.00:1,
      reverse 3.63:1
    (1300)   3.52:1, 2.22:1, 1.43:1, 1.00:1,
      reverse 3.54:1

   (1300GT)   3.30:1, 2.07:1, 1.35:1, 1.00:1,
      reverse 3.35:1
Four-speed AP automatic gearbox optional from
October 1965; gear ratios 2.69:1, 1.85:1, 1.46:1, 1,00:1,
reverse 2.69.
Front-wheel drive

Axle ratio
1100: 4.13:1
1300: 3.65:1
Austin America: 3.76:1

Suspension, steering and brakes
All-round independent suspension with Hydrolastic
units, interconnected front to rear. Front suspension
with wishbones; rear suspension with trailing arms and
anti-roll bar
Rack-and-pinion steering
Front disc brakes and rear drum brakes. Servo
standard on export 1300GT and optional in the UK

Dimensions

Overall length	12ft 2.7in (3,726mm)
Overall width	5ft 0.4in (1534mm)
Overall height	4ft 4.7in (1,338mm)
Wheelbase	7ft 9.5in (2,375mm)
Front track	4ft 3.5in (1,308mm)
Rear track	4ft 2.9in (1,292mm)

Wheels and tyres
12-inch steel disc wheels, with 4-inch rims
5.50 × 12 cross-ply tyres
5.95 × 12 crossply tyres (Austin America)
145 × 12 radial tyres (available from 1968)

Unladen weights

1100 Mk I 4-door	1,800lb (817kg) approx
1100 Mk II 2-door	1,768lb (802kg)
1100 Mk II 4-door	1,827lb (829kg)
1300 Mk II 2-door	1,815lb (823kg)
1300 Mk II 4-door	1,844lb (836kg)
1300GT	1,900lb (863kg) approx

Performance and fuel

1100

0–60mph	22.2 sec
Maximum	78mph (125.3km/h)
Fuel consumption	33mpg (8.58ltr/100km)

1300

0–60mph	17.3 sec
Maximum	88mph (141.6km/h)
Fuel consumption	30mpg (9.43ltr/100km)

1300GT

0–60mph	15.6 sec
Maximum	93mph (149.6km/h)
Fuel consumption	27mpg (10.48ltr/100km)

AUSTIN AND MORRIS 1100 AND 1300 MK II AND MK III IDENTIFICATION NUMBERS

Car numbers ('chassis' or VIN numbers)

A A2SA	Austin 1100 or 1300, Mk II or Mk III, two-door
A ASA	Austin 1100 or 1300, Mk II or Mk III, four-door
A A4DA	Austin 1300GT
A A2SU	Austin America, 1968
A A2SAU	Austin America, 1968
A A2SD	Austin America, 1969
A A2SDU	Austin America, 1969
A A2SDUA	Austin America, 1970
A A2SDUB	Austin America, 1970
M A2S2	Morris 1100 or 1300, Mk II, two-door
M AS2	Morris 1100 or 1300 Mk II, four-door
M A4D2	Morris 1300GT

These prefix codes may be followed by an L for LHD models. On Mk II and Mk III models, a D in this position denotes a De Luxe model, and an S denotes a Super De Luxe type. Next comes the serial number, which is followed by an A (Longbridge assembly) or an M (Cowley assembly). A full number might therefore read M A2S2L 56789 A.

Commission numbers

2 16 2S	Austin 1100 or 1300 Mk II, two-door
2 16 S	Austin 1100 or 1300 Mk II, four-door
3 16 2S	Austin 1100 or 1300, Mk III, two-door
3 16 S	Austin 1100 or 1300, Mk III, four-door
2 16 4D	Austin 1300GT
AU 16 2S	Austin America, 1968–1969
AU 16 2SA	Austin America, 1970
AU 16 2 SB	Austin America, 1971
2 16 2S	Morris 1100 or 1300, Mk II, two-door
2 16 S	Morris 1100 or 1300, Mk II, four-door
3 16 2S	Morris 1100 or 1300, Mk III, two-door
3 16 S	Morris 1100 or 1300, Mk III, four-door
2 16 4D	Morris 1300GT

These prefix codes are followed by the serial number, which in turn is followed by an A, an L or an M on some Mk II models. Both A and L appear to indicate assembly at Longbridge, while the M indicates assembly at Cowley.

AUSTIN AND MORRIS 1100 AND 1300 MK II AND MK III IDENTIFICATION NUMBERS *continued*

Body shell numbers

B2S	Austin or Morris Mk II or Mk III two-door De Luxe
2S	Austin or Morris Mk II or Mk III two-door Super De Luxe
BS	Austin or Morris Mk II or Mk III four-door De Luxe
S	Austin or Morris Mk II or Mk III four-door Super De Luxe
4D	Austin or Morris 1300GT

These prefix codes are followed by the serial number, which in turn is followed by the letter A, L or P. A and L appear to indicate Longbridge build, while P indicates Cowley. A full number might therefore read B2S 12345 P.

Engine codes

10H	Austin or Morris 1100 Mk II and Mk III
12H	Austin or Morris 1300 Mk II and Mk III

On Mk II and Mk III models, the engine prefix code is followed by a four-digit code consisting of three numbers and a letter. Typical would be 354E, which indicates mechanical fuel pump, crankcase ventilation, Lucas 16AC alternator and a standard-ratio gearbox. The H or L code then prefixes the serial number, so that a typical number might be 10H354E-H12345.

AUSTIN AND MORRIS 1100 AND 1300 PRODUCTION, MK I, MK II AND MK III

These production figures are for calendar-years, and were provided by the manufacturer during its time as the Austin Rover Group. Austin and Morris figures can be separated for the period up to and including 1969, but thereafter the figures for the two marques are combined.

The 1966 Export figures may include export two-door models.

The 1967 figures include both Mk I and Mk II models, which cannot currently be split accurately. The 1967–9 figures are cumulative totals for both two-door and four-door models.

The 1968 and later figures for the Austin 1300 probably include the Austin America, of which approximately 58,500 were built in all.

Austin, 1963–9

Year	Home	Export	Total	
1963	17,495	10,592	28,087	(4-door)
1964	82,332	27,189	109,521	(4-door)
1965	72,646	27,546	100,192	(4-door)
1966	62,209	25,620	87,829	(4-door)
1967	56,945	20,871	77,816	(1100)
	440	253	693	(1300)
1968	37,249	16,927	54,176	(1100)
	22,723	37,077	59,800	(1300)
1969	27,241	14,751	41,992	(1100)
	38,047	43,143	81,190	(1300)
	2,876	484	3,360	(1300GT)
	Grand Total		644,656	

Morris, 1962–9

Year	Home	Export	Total	
1962	12,554	7531	20,085	(4-door)
	0	199	199	(2-door)
1963	63,625	37,804	101,429	(4-door)
	0	9	9	(2-door)
1964	70,629	28,589	98,858	(4-door)
	0	0	0	(2-door)
1965	58,945	22,241	81,186	(4-door)
	0	30	30	(2-door)
1966	55,028	13,885	68,913	(4-door)
	0	2,542	2,542	(2-door)
1967	47,420	14,178	61,598	(1100)
	414	308	722	(1300)
1968	30,061	14,473	44,534	(1100)
	20,616	14,466	35,082	(1300)
1969	21,417	9395	30,812	(1100)
	32,644	15,347	47,991	(1300)
	2,588	635	3,223	(1300GT)
		Grand Total	597,213	

The 1967 figures include both Mk I and Mk II models, which cannot currently be split accurately. The 1967–9 figures are cumulative totals for both two-door and four-door models.

Austin and Morris, 1970–75

Year	Home	Export	Total	
1970	17,882	6,809	24,691	(1100 2-door)
	25,654	10,208	35,862	(1100 4-door)
	9,645	15,965	25,610	(1300 2-door)
	47,898	25,468	73,366	(1300 4-door)
	11,274	5,883	17,157	(1300GT)
1971	13,641	9,104	22,745	(1100 2-door)
	18,035	5,944	23,979	(1100 4-door)
	7,499	12,395	19,894	(1300 2-door)
	39,159	28,791	67,950	(1300 4-door)
	11,145	8,809	19,954	(1300GT)
1972	10,598	4,468	15,066	(1100 2-door)
	11,752	3,604	15,356	(1100 4-door)
	5,350	2,750	8100	(1300 2-door)
	41,805	11,473	53,278	(1300 4-door)
	10,806	7,360	18,166	(1300GT)
1973	5,512	4,604	10,116	(1100 2-door)
	4,546	3,171	7,717	(1100 4-door)
	2,897	3,130	6,027	(1300 2-door)
	16,601	13,814	30,415	(1300 4-door)
	3,033	5,903	8,936	(1300GT)
1974	0	1,631	1,631	(1100 2-door)
	0	2,058	2,058	(1100 4-door)
	0	2,076	2,076	(1300 2-door)
	1,742	12,237	13,979	(1300 4-door)
	243	670	913	(1300GT)
1975	0	1,788	1,788	(1300 4-door)
		Grand Total	526,830	

The 1971 figures cover both Mk II and Mk III models. The individual figures cannot currently be determined.

The 1975 figures were probably all CKD cars; UK production of ADO16 ended in June 1974.

The overall production total for Austin and Morris saloon derivatives of the ADO16 models was 1,768,699. Of these, well over 1.1 million were 1100 models and just under 600,000 were 1300s.

CHAPTER FOUR

ESTATES:
THE PRACTICAL MODELS

Estate cars had been gaining in popularity throughout the 1950s in Britain. Although they had been uncommon before the Second World War, and in those days generally confined to such places as shooting estates (hence the name) and based on larger chassis to give maximum carrying capacity, they had gained a new popularity from the late 1940s. One reason was that estate bodies were not subject to Purchase Tax as long as they met certain criteria; another was perhaps the influence of America, where the capacious multi-purpose station wagon (the US name) was increasingly becoming a feature of suburban life.

One way or another, all the major British manufacturers introduced estate cars in the 1950s, and BMC was among the leaders in the field. There were estate derivatives of most models in its Austin and Morris ranges by the end of the decade, and even Mini estates appeared in 1962 alongside the first of the 1100s: it was clear right from the start that there would sooner or later be an estate derivative of the ADO16 range.

BMC, however, took their time about getting one into production. The Morris Minor 1000 was still selling well in 'woody' estate form in the early 1960s, and the similarly engined Austin A40 Countryman with its early version of a hatchback configuration styled by Pininfarina was keeping the Austin dealers happy. The Minor was already seen as an evergreen product, and there were no plans to withdraw it, but the A40 was a standalone car in the BMC range, with no badge-engineered versions. In the interests of

long-overdue rationalization, it would have to go soon. In fact, it went in 1967, just a year after estate versions of the ADO16 range had been introduced.

At this stage in Britain, estate cars were expected to have only two doors, leaving the area behind the front seats unobstructed by such things as armrests and window-winders that would get in the way of the folding rear seat. So the ADO16 estate was designed as a two-door car, like other BMC estates of the period. All the work seems to have been done at Longbridge, and the Austin Drawing Office deserves a great deal of credit for creating a design that flowed smoothly and did not look – as did so many estate models of the 1960s and later – as if it was a crude conversion of the saloon.

Although the basic lines of the saloons were retained, as indeed was the 93.5-inch wheelbase, a good deal of new sheet metal was designed for the estates. The rear floor had to be redesigned to give a flat load area and new extended rear wings had to be drawn up. Fortunately for BMC's costings, it was possible to retain the saloon's tail light units. However, a new and longer roof panel was required, and new side windows, arranged to slide open within their frames, had to be designed as well. These incorporated plastic locking catches, with a peg that engaged in a channel at the bottom of the frame.

On top of that, the fuel tank had to be redesigned so that it did not compromise the flat floor, and its filler was recessed into the left-hand rear wing, where it sat several inches further back than

Estates looked a little plain from the side, but the customers didn't worry about that. The longer roofline provided more stowage space in the back, although the overall length was no greater than that of the saloon. The large side windows slid open to improve ventilation. That registration plate of **CFC 4D** appeared on other **ADO16** cars used for publicity pictures, as well.

The one-piece tailgate that was adopted for production. The badge made no reference to the fact that this was an estate version of the companion saloon.

on the equivalent saloons. The rear seat had to be redesigned so that it would fold forwards. Finally, a new tailgate had to be designed. It looks as if the original plan was to have a split tailgate – certainly a mock-up or prototype car was built with one – but this was considered too heavy and a one-piece, counterbalanced top-hinged tailgate was designed for production.

CRAYFORD ESTATES

The four-year delay between the introduction of the 1100 saloons and the arrival of estate derivatives prompted Crayford to develop their own estate model. In practice, this was very different from the BMC-built estate and retained the overall body shape of the standard saloon. It was announced in January 1965, some fifteen months before the factory-built models were introduced.

The press demonstrator, which was presumably also the first conversion, was based on an MG 1100. Central to the conversion was a split tailgate, which retained the drop-down boot lid of the original car and supplemented it with a hatchback that contained the rear window. This was made of aluminium, with hinges at the top, supporting struts and its own lifting handle. The standard rear seat was modified to allow it to fold in traditional estate-car style (the rear doors had to be opened first), and the load area was tidied up by the addition of lining panels for the body sides and a rubber floor mat. The butchery of the rear pillars was concealed by a vinyl cover trim, in a colour contrasting with the bodywork, and on this Crayford mounted their own badge.

The Crayford 'estate' was really more of a hatchback. This example was based on a 1965 Austin 1100 and shows how the basic lines of the saloon remained intact. On the rear pillar, the modifications to the metalwork were concealed under a cover panel that carried the Crayford name. This was a 'de luxe' version, with painted rear window surround; on standard models, the panel was left in unpainted aluminium.

In basic form the conversion cost £79. For £115, there was a 'de luxe' version, with the rear window surround painted to match the bodywork, a carpeted load area with longitudinal protective strips and an automatic courtesy light for the load area. This was something of a bargain, not least because the car was an aftermarket conversion and therefore not subject to the Purchase Tax levied on new cars. Crayford were happy to convert either a brand-new car or one which had already seen a period of use.

Crayford's business was expanding rapidly in the mid-1960s and the company was still operating out of the homes of its directors. Construction of the 1100 estate was sub-contracted to FLM Panelcraft in London and, according to AROnline, also to Methven & Thomas in Fife. Each conversion is said to have taken eight days to complete.

No fewer than thirty BMC dealers agreed to handle conversions, although it is likely that many of them never actually sold any. In fact, the total number built is simply not known. The Crayford Convertible Car Club has traced just two in addition to the MG 1100 demonstrator, one based on a Vanden Plas Princess and the other on a Wolseley 1300. Only the Wolseley is still thought to survive.

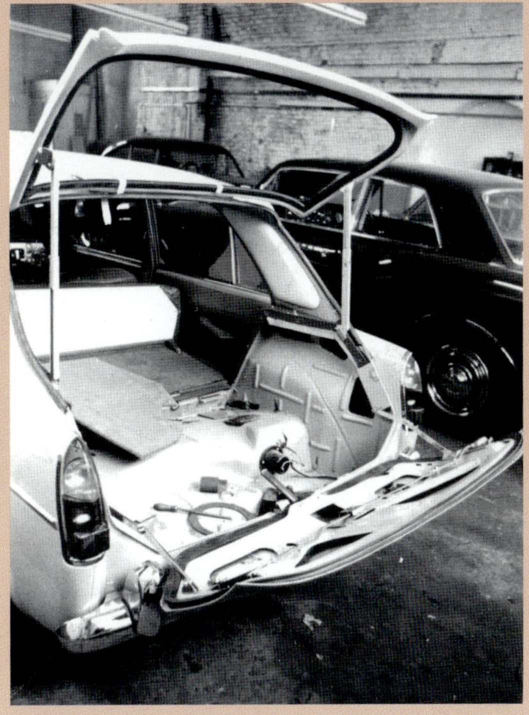

ABOVE RIGHT AND BOTTOM: **The load area in the Crayford conversion was also impressively large, although of course it lacked the length at roof height that the BMC estate provided. The press car, seen here under construction, was built at the premises of FLM Panelcraft in Fulham, with whom Crayford had a working arrangement.**

In theory, the ADO16 estate shell could have been dressed and equipped to represent any one of the six marques of which saloon versions existed. In practice, however, BMC considered that estate cars were 'family' vehicles, so there was no point in creating sporting MG and Riley or luxury Vanden Plas and Wolseley versions. Even so, Vanden Plas did build two prototype Princess estates, of which no production followed. Just two versions of the estate – Austin and Morris – were announced when the new models were introduced at the Geneva Motor Show in March 1966. Shown with them was a cutaway Austin derivative that showed the interior layout; known as the 'Skeleton', this

Many a slip … early thinking at BMC was to give the estates a split tailgate, and the design was tried out on a mock-up or prototype. Sadly, weight counted against it and a one-piece tailgate was used instead. The side trim-strip seen on this car was not carried over to production, unfortunately.

OPPOSITE BOTTOM AND RIGHT: **This 'skeleton' Austin Countryman estate was displayed at the Geneva Motor Show, and then again at Earls Court in 1967. The front and rear seats could be moved by electric motors, to demonstrate the versatility of the load space. After many years in storage, the cutaway was rescued and restored by Roy Maskrey of RPM Workshops in Chesterfield. It now belongs to The 1100 Club and is normally displayed at the Stondon Transport Museum.**

still survives and at the time of writing belonged to the 1100 Club and was displayed in the Stondon Transport Museum at Lower Stondon, Henlow, in Bedfordshire.

The new Austin and Morris estates took familiar names from the traditions of each marque. The Austin became an 1100 Countryman and the Morris an 1100 Traveller. Interestingly, neither had the wooden appliqué strips associated with other BMC estates of the time; both Austin and Morris came with unadorned panelwork, and looked all the better for it. In fact, no evidence has come to light that the 'woody' look was ever considered for these cars, and no later BMC estates had it, either, even though Mk II models would have an appliqué fake-wood strip along their sides. Presumably, BMC considered that the wood-framed look had become too old-fashioned by this time.

On the inside there were no surprises. The dashboard and front seats were identical with those of the equivalent saloons and the upholstery style was the same, too. Probably few customers bemoaned the loss of the rear ashtray, which had to go so that the seat could fold forwards. That seat could also fold backwards, and the point of that became apparent a couple of months after the Geneva launch. In May 1967 the reclining front seat option was introduced for the ADO16 range, and when that was specified for an estate, it was possible to fold all the seats flat to make a reasonably sized, if somewhat lumpy, double bed in the car.

Although saloon production was spread between Cowley and Longbridge, all estate assembly was centred on Longbridge. The Austin plant had become what would now be called a centre of excellence for estate production, and so both Austin and Morris 1100 estates were built there. Similar arrangements had been made for the production of Mini estates. However, a considerable amount of pre-assembly was done at the Fisher & Ludlow plant in Castle Bromwich. Fisher & Ludlow not only pressed the panels for the estates, but

ABOVE AND LEFT: **The tailgate gave a wide opening to facilitate loading, and the space inside was as big as most owners ever needed, especially when the rear seats were folded forwards.**

also assembled, painted and trimmed the bodies, adding glass, trim, electrical components and lights before sending the completed assemblies to Longbridge. There the mechanical underpinnings were assembled to the cars on the same assembly lines that were used for the Mini estates in the assembly hall known as CABI (the initials stood for Car Assembly Building).

PRESS VIEWS OF THE 1100 ESTATES

In the UK, BMC did not provide test cars for the press until autumn 1966, and the two leading weekly publications tried examples in the same week during October. *Autocar* magazine tested a Morris 1100 Traveller for its issue of 28 October 1966, and *Motor* tried an Austin 1100 Countryman for its issue dated 29 October. Opinions were mixed.

The *Autocar* test car arrived with a number of faults and had to be sent back for some of them to be corrected. Both performance and fuel consumption turned out to be very close to those of the equivalent saloon, but the magazine had its doubts about a number of aspects of the new car.

The stiffer suspension gave a ride that was 'quite firm, with quite harsh reactions to sudden bumps and ruts'. However, a load of about 3.5cwt of ballast (392lb or 188kg) in the rear barely affected the handling, 'and there was still far more cornering power available than we could use without shifting our cargo'. Heavy braking caused the load to shift forwards, of course, and the rear seat backrest tipped forwards under the strain. The rear-seat folding arrangement was also thought to be 'complicated and often inconvenient', despite its ability to be turned into a bed in tandem with the optional reclining front seats. As the tipping front seats were also liable to movement under heavy braking, 'we consider the seating arrangement of the Traveller to be of poor design'.

The car was noisy, too:

Generally, the noise level in the Traveller is very high, and is rather tiring on motorways. There is a lot of commotion at the front under one's feet (where all the running gear is) above about 30mph, and at 70mph conversation becomes strained. Some of the noise is a not-unpleasant gear whine, but most of it is tyre roar and a deep, resonant body rumble which booms about inside.

The magazine concluded that 'some improvements to the interior layout and trim quality should be high on the manufacturer's list of priorities, as well as some attention to safety features'.

The *Motor* report was rather more positive, and the magazine thought that the Countryman or its Morris equivalent offered enough additional features to be 'excellent value for the £712 asked'. The magazine approved of the versatility of the rear seat arrangement, pointing out that the seat could be laid flat so that tired children could rest in the back, 'whereas with a conventional non-reclining rear seat, quarrels tend to ensue from attempts to lie across it'. (It would still be some years before allowing children to travel in the back like this would become illegal.)

Handling was excellent, as with the saloon, although 'press-on drivers should be warned that the car can oversteer and become quite tail-happy – especially in the wet – if a heavy load is carried at the extreme rear'. Noise levels were certainly high, 'but the level is no higher than in the saloon: it has not been accentuated by the estate car body'.

Worth noting is that the car went down well overseas, too. *Car South Africa* tested a locally assembled Austin 1100 Countryman for its October 1967 issue, and summarized that 'the smaller station wagon fills a vital role as an economical, handy, versatile family car, and in this capacity, the Countryman has strong capabilities. In fact, 'these almost flawless little family transports suffer only from rather high pricing'.

THE VANS

Just as BMC had developed estate and van derivatives of the Mini with a common body shell (albeit with some hiccups along the way), so the company believed it could develop a small van from the estate version of the ADO16. Plans for this were under way by the late summer of 1964, at which stage there were thoughts of using leaf-spring suspension in place of the Hydrolastic system.

Just over three years later, in November 1967, a prototype batch of vans was built. However, thoughts of using leaf-spring suspension had been abandoned by this stage, and the fifty vehicles all had the same Hydrolastic system as the saloons and estates. It appears that these were built to 1100 Mk II standard, as their instrument panels had a single large dial similar to that used on the Mk II De Luxe models of the 1100 and 1300. Nevertheless, they seem to have been built without the side repeater indicators that characterized the Mk II estates.

Some at least carried Austin badges; whether any of them wore Morris badges is not clear. Some of them were sent to BMC dealers for what must have been considered to be field trials, and they were pressed into service as parts delivery vans. The 1100 Club reports that twenty-two vans went to ShellMex BP for similar evaluation by that company's service engineers. The known examples from this batch of fifty acquired E- and F-suffix registration numbers, dating from 1967 and, perhaps, early 1968.

One example was tested by *Motor Transport* magazine for its March 1968 issue. This van had covered 9,000 miles from new and was in daily use carrying parts from stores to distributors and to airports. The magazine reported that the van was noticeably quiet, and that the Hydrolastic suspension helped to damp out road noise. One delivery driver who regularly travelled to Scotland in one of these vans said that he could do 400 miles at speeds up to 70mph without fatigue. At well over 30mpg, fuel consumption was excellent.

The major drawback, as BMC engineers had clearly anticipated in 1964, was that the Hydrolastic suspension did not take kindly to heavy loads in the van body. Heavy weights in the back caused the rear suspension units to compress, transferring the load to the front ones, which then lifted the nose. Alex Moulton became involved in work to develop a limiting device that would cure this problem (which was of course shared with the estates), but nothing further came of it and no van production ever followed.

None of that prevented some small businesses from using 1100 (and, later, 1300) estates as vans, folding the rear seats down or removing them altogether and adding signwritten boards to cover the long side windows. This ploy was not only adopted by small businesses: television rental company DER did exactly the same.

THE JENSEN CONVERTIBLE

Jensen Motors of West Bromwich was going through a tricky financial period in 1967, and it seems probable that the company began to cast about for additional revenue streams. In June that year the company bought an Austin 1100 Countryman (number A-AW10-16279A) and turned it into the prototype of a convertible. An estate model was chosen presumably because its two-door configuration was better suited than the four-door saloon to the planned convertible configuration; no two-door saloon was available on the UK market at the time.

The car was displayed on Jensen's stand at the Earls Court Motor Show in October 1967, although it was not listed in the official catalogue of the event. This suggests that its inclusion alongside examples of the Jensen Interceptor and FF coupés was a last-minute addition. Finished in Alaskan Blue with blue upholstery, the car seems to have been the only example produced. Later registered as LEA 765E, it was sold to a Jensen dealership and presumably passed into public ownership. It is not clear whether the car still survives.

THE MK II MODELS, 1967–71

Just as the original 1100 saloons were superseded by Mk II models in October 1967, so the estates gave way to Mk II models. There were no great surprises about the specification. The body shells were the same as before, retaining the Mk I style of tail lamps and not taking on the more raked style of lamps used on the saloons. Wheels were all painted silver in the latest BMC corporate style (the Mk II Minis introduced at the same time had the same feature). Like the saloons, the estates now had side repeater indicators on the front wings. They also had simulated wood-grain bodyside mouldings in bright metal frames. These did help to reduce the plainness of the Mk I estates, but the 'wood' was so obviously fake that it tended to have a cheapening effect on the appearance. Inside the cars, the configuration was the same as before, although the Mk II models had the new style of seat trim also seen on Mk II saloons.

The Austin 1100 Countryman Mk II and Morris 1100 Traveller Mk II shared their new tailgate badges with the Mk II saloons, and their tailgates also carried the chrome script 'Mk II' badge that was seen on Minis at the same time. Just like the saloons, the Countryman and Traveller were now available with the larger 1275cc engine as well, when they were badged as 1300 models. The larger-engined cars did not have these 'Mk II' badges because they were not the second iteration of their type. Knowing how BMC worked at the time, it would also be true to say that not putting these badges on the cars was welcomed as a way of saving money!

In fact, the 1300 versions of the two estates went down so well that for some countries, including the UK, the 1100 Mk II was discontinued after just six months, in March 1968. From that point on, there were just 1275cc models of the Austin and the Morris, and they remained in production until a third iteration of the estate design was introduced in 1971. Prices were gradually creeping up in this period. When the estates had first appeared at the Earls Court Motor Show in October 1966, they had both been listed at £711 11s 3d (£577 10s 0d plus £134 1s 3d Purchase Tax) without extras. A year later, the new Mk II models were listed at £769 19s 0d (£625 plus £144 19s 0d Purchase Tax) – a price hike perhaps masked by the change to Mk II specification. However, at the 1968 Show the Countryman had gone up yet again, this time to £826 5s 0d (£645 plus £181 5s 0d Purchase Tax).

A side trim-strip did appear on the Mk II estate models, although it was rather different from the slim metal type tried out earlier. Mk IIs had indicator repeater lamps on the front wings and, of course, perforated wheel discs. This is a Morris 1300 Traveller.

This was the interior of the Mk III Traveller, with the vacuum-formed vinyl seats characteristic of the period, the redesigned steering wheel and twin round dials set in a wood-effect facia panel. The overall effect was quite pleasing.

PRESS VIEWS OF THE 1300 ESTATES

The mainstream UK motoring press seems not to have been interested in testing examples of the new 1300 estates; they focused on the saloons and allowed readers to draw their own conclusions about the estates, which after all offered only the new engine over what had been tested before. So it was left to the Automobile Association's *Drive* magazine to provide some contemporary comment in its Autumn 1968 issue.

The AA commented that 'the smooth and flexible engine responds with brisk acceleration and a top speed of 85mph. At 70mph the car is running at 600rpm fewer than the 1100, and overall fuel consumption at 35.2mpg is 1mpg better.' The usual ADO16 traits of excellent suspension comfort and 'outstandingly' safe roadholding were highlighted, but the magazine also noted that there were no safety catches on the tip-up front seats. The road test was finished off by comments from 1300 estate owner Geoffrey Whittaker, a 52-year-old male nurse who had earlier owned a Morris 1100. They are worth quoting in full:

I am a keen sea angler and really bought the 1300 to hold all my fishing gear. The improvements over the 1100 are impressive and I particularly like the higher seating position. It makes me feel more in command.

There have been some small faults – a petrol leak, a badly fitting door and a loose speedometer cable. There is also a rattle in the back seat.

The acceleration, speed and overall performance have all been up to expectations. My wife doesn't drive, but she likes the new car for the better acceleration and smooth ride, and finds the interior comfortable and roomy. The interior light over the cargo space is especially useful when loading up for a fishing trip early in the morning.

However, *Autocar* did run an interesting comparison test between the Austin 1300 Countryman and one of its obvious rivals, the Ford Escort 1300 estate, in its issue of 6 August 1970. There was no clear winner and the Austin held up well against the much newer rear-wheel-drive Ford design. Stuart Bladon concluded that he liked the Austin better overall, but that it still had the same faults that the ADO16 saloons had exhibited in 1962. The Ford had inferior roadholding and steering, but 'it really is pretty good and not all that behind in these respects. It also has appreciably more engine refinement and a nicer gearbox.' In the end, 'I choose the Escort, with the proviso that it would only take some elementary updating of the Austin to make me prefer that instead.'

Bladon's colleague Michael Scarlett favoured the Ford for its greater load capacity, but the Austin for its passenger accommodation: 'I would in any case value the Austin's very much better performance and generally better road behaviour; its absolute surefootedness is delightful.' Even so, the Ford had better ventilation and heating, a quieter transmission, a better gear change and lighter controls.

THE MK III MODELS, 1971–4

The estates entered the Mk III era in September 1971 at the same time as the saloons. There were only 1275cc '1300' derivatives by this time, but in the beginning both Austin and Morris versions were available. The Morris 1300 Traveller Mk III, however, threatened to clash with the new Morris Marina estate, which would be introduced in 1972, and so it was withdrawn from sale in the UK in April that year, remaining available in export markets for just one more year. The Austin 1300 Countryman Mk III then continued in production

for another fourteen months, the last one being built in June 1974.

Like the saloons, the 1300 Countryman had a three-bar grille with a black background and a '1300' badge, and of course a distinguishing badge on the tailgate and a single British Leyland emblem on the left-hand front wing. The same signs of cost-cutting were present, too, as the Mk III estates had no over-riders, no side repeater indicators, no front door pockets and (uniquely for the estates) only one lock instead of two on their sliding side windows. As for prices, the 1300 Countryman cost £976.88, which broke down as £780 plus £196.88 Purchase Tax, on its introduction.

The same new dashboard was in evidence, too, with two circular dials set in a full-depth fake wood facia that incorporated a glovebox, an ashtray and a pair of swivelling air vents in its ends. The steering wheel was now a 15-inch size, there was a new plastic gear knob, and the foot pedals were larger than before. Heater and fan controls now had plastic moulded bodies (mainly to meet new safety legislation in some export markets), and the sun visors were smaller. The front seats were wider than before and both front and rear seats were upholstered in vinyl with heat-formed horizontal pleats – a benefit in manufacturing terms but a retrograde step in aesthetic terms. The carpet, at least, was thicker than before.

Mk III 1300 estate with the new blacked-out grille. There was no British Leyland badge on this side of the car.

PAINT AND TRIM COLOURS – AUSTIN

1100 Countryman Mk I (1966–7)

Body	Interior
Black	Peony Red
Cumulus Grey	Fresco Blue or Peony Red
El Paso Beige	Adam Beige
Maroon B	Satin Beige
Trafalgar Blue	Fresco Blue

Austin 1100 Countryman Mk II (1967–71)
Austin 1300 Countryman Mk II (1967–71)

Body	Interior
Alaskan Blue	Fresco Blue
Black	Peony Red
Cumulus Grey	Peony Red
El Paso Beige	Adam Beige
Snowberry White	Black
Tartan Red	Black
Trafalgar Blue	Fresco Blue

Austin 1100 Countryman Mk III (1971–4)
Austin 1300 Countryman Mk III (1971–4)

Body	Interior
Aqua	Navy
Black Tulip	Geranium
Blaze	Navy
Bronze Yellow	Navy
Flame Red	Navy
Glacier White	Autumn Leaf or Navy
Green Mallard	Limeflower
Harvest Gold	Olive
Limeflower	Limeflower
Midnight Blue	Geranium or Navy
Teal Blue	Limeflower

PAINT AND TRIM COLOURS – MORRIS

1100 Traveller Mk I (1966–7)

Body	Interior
Black	Peony Red
Cumulus Grey	Fresco Blue or Peony Red
Maroon B	Satin Beige
Trafalgar Blue	Fresco Blue

1100 Traveller Mk II (1967–71)
1300 Traveller Mk II (1967–71)

Body	Interior
Black	Peony Red
Connaught Green	Porcelain Green
Sandy Beige	Peony Red
Smoke Grey	Blue-Grey
Snowberry White	Black
Tartan Red	Peony Red
Trafalgar Blue	Fresco Blue

1100 Traveller Mk III (1971–4)
1300 Traveller Mk III (1971–4)

Body	Interior
Aqua	Navy
Black Tulip	Geranium or Navy
Blaze	Navy
Bronze Yellow	Navy
Damask Red	Navy
Flame Red	Navy
Glacier White	Autumn Leaf, Geranium, Navy or Olive
Green Mallard	Limeflower
Harvest Gold	Olive
Limeflower	Limeflower or Navy
Midnight Blue	Geranium or Navy
Teal Blue	Limeflower or Olive

Technical Specifications, Austin and Morris ADO16 Estates

Engine
1100 models
BMC A-series 4-cylinder, with iron block and cylinder
head
1098cc (64.58 × 83.72mm)
Overhead valves; chain-driven camshaft
Three-bearing crankshaft
Compression ratio 8.5:1
One SU HS2 carburettor (manual gearbox models) or
one SU HS4 carburettor (automatic models)
48bhp at 5,100rpm
60 lb ft at 2,500rpm

1300 models
BMC A-series 4-cylinder, with iron block and
cylinder head
1275cc (70.6 × 81.28mm)
Overhead valves; chain-driven camshaft
Three-bearing crankshaft
Compression ratio 8.8:1
One SU HS4 carburettor
58bhp at 5,250rpm
69 lb ft at 3,000rpm

Transmission
Four-speed manual gearbox, with no synchromesh on
first gear with synchromesh on all forward gears from
mid-1968
Gear ratios (1100)   3.63:1, 2.17:1, 1.41:1, 1.00:1,
                    reverse 3.63:1
            (1300)   3.52:1, 2.22:1, 1.43:1, 1.00:1,
                    reverse 3.54:1
Front-wheel drive

Axle ratio
1100: 4.13:1
1300: 3.65:1

Suspension, steering and brakes
All-round independent suspension with Hydrolastic
units, interconnected front to rear. Front suspension
with wishbones; rear suspension with trailing arms and
anti-roll bar
Rack-and-pinion steering
Front disc brakes and rear drum brakes

Dimensions
Overall length	12ft 2.7in (3,726mm)
Overall width	5ft 0.4in (1,534mm)
Overall height	4ft 4.7in (1,338mm)
Wheelbase	7ft 9.5in (2,375mm)
Front track	4ft 3.5in (1,308mm)
Rear track	4ft 2.9in (1,292mm)

Wheels and tyres
12-inch steel disc wheels, with 4-inch rims
5.50 × 12 cross-ply tyres
145 × 12 radial tyres (available from 1968)

Unladen weights
1100 models	1,855lb (842kg) approx
Mk II 1300	1,881lb (853kg) approx

Performance and fuel
1100
0–60mph	22.9 sec
Maximum	80mph (128.7km/h)
Fuel consumption	31mpg (9.13ltr/100km)

1300
0–60mph	18.6 sec
Maximum	88mph (141.6km/h)
Fuel consumption	33mpg (8.58ltr/100km)

The estates were replaced in the British Leyland line-up by the Morris Marina estate and the Austin Allegro estate. By this stage, British Leyland was trying to make a clear distinction between the Austin and Morris marques, and the new policy was to characterize Austin by modern technology (such as front-wheel drive) and striking styling (questionable in the Allegro's case), while Morris became the conventional marque (with rear-wheel drive and unadventurous styling).

PRODUCTION FIGURES FOR AUSTIN 1100 AND 1300 COUNTRYMAN, AND MORRIS 1100 AND 1300 TRAVELLER

These production figures are for calendar-years, and were provided by the manufacturer during its time as the Austin Rover Group. Austin and Morris figures can be separated for the period up to and including 1969, but thereafter the figures for the two marques are combined.

Austin, 1966–9

Year	Home	Export	Total	
1966	3,684	1,852	5,536	
1967	9,242	1,088	10,330	(1100)
	1	0	1	(1300)
1968	35	730	765	(1100)
	3,896	701	4,597	(1300)
1969	15	186	201	(1100)
	5,507	860	6,367	(1300)
		Grand Total	27,797	

The 1967 figures include both Mk I and Mk II models, which cannot currently be split accurately.

Morris, 1966–9

Year	Home	Export	Total	
1966	3,627	1,521	5,148	
1967	7,422	598	8,020	(1100)
	5	2	7	(1300)
1968	77	232	309	(1100)
	3,678	516	4,194	(1300)
1969	74	119	193	(1100)
	5,430	1,186	6,616	(1300)
	Grand Total	24,487		

The 1967 figures include both Mk I and Mk II models, which cannot currently be split accurately.

Austin and Morris, 1970–74

Year	Home	Export	Total	
1970	9,025	1,752	10,777	(1300)
1971	11,885	1,315	13,200	(1300)
1972	11,380	1,310	12,690	(1300)
1973	9,489	886	10,375	(1300)
1974	1,479	71	1,550	(1300)
	Grand Total	48,592		

The 1971 figures cover both Mk II and Mk III models. The individual figures cannot currently be determined.

The overall production total for estate derivatives of the ADO16 models was 100,876. Of these, 30,502 were 1100 models and 70,374 were 1300s.

AUSTIN AND MORRIS ESTATES: IDENTIFICATION NUMBERS

The vehicle identification numbers for the Countryman and Traveller estates follow the same pattern as those for Austin and Morris saloons, except that the third group in the prefix code (S or 2S on the saloons) is replaced by 2W. A similar substitution occurs for the Commission Numbers and Body Shell Numbers. Engine codes are the same as those for saloon models.

CHAPTER FIVE

MG AND RILEY: THE SPORTY MODELS

BMC put the first of their sporty ADO16 derivatives on the market before they had even completed the core range with the Austin version. In October 1962, less than two months after the Morris 1100 had been released, an MG 1100 was announced as a companion model.

Interestingly, the car might have been badged as an MGC 1100; it was introduced just a few days after the new MGB sports car had been introduced, and David Knowles (in *MG – The Untold Story*) tells of a document that calls it exactly that. It appears that the name was vetoed by MG at Abingdon because they wanted to keep the letter designations for their sports cars. So an MG 1100 it became.

Note that a model called the MG Princess was briefly available in the USA. This was an MG-badged version of the Vanden Plas 1100, and is covered with the other Vanden Plas models in Chapter 5.

MG 1100 MK 1

Ever since their first use in 1924, the letters MG had stood for a sporting model based on a more mundane Morris, and the new car was planned to continue that tradition. To deliver better performance than the Morris 1100, it therefore had a twin-carburettor version of the 1098cc engine with double valve springs, delivering 55bhp and rather more lively acceleration up to a heady top speed of 85mph. More than that, however, had to remain in the driver's imagination for the moment.

There were, of course, multiple cosmetic differences between Morris and MG. Not the least of these was a completely different front end design, arranged around a traditional MG grille and with circular combination units for the sidelights and direction indicators. While the MG octagon on the grille was in red (as on the latest MGB), it appeared in black on the hubcaps and on the boot lid. Then, while the Morris was available only in single paint colours, the MG could be had in fashionable duotones as well. To this end, each side had a bright trim strip along the body crease, where it served as a colour boundary; on the boot, a further bright finisher performed the same function. The boot finisher also served to make the boot handle look different at first sight, although it was in fact the same fluted type as on the Morris 1100.

For the home market the MG 1100 came exclusively as a four-door saloon, but BMC's transatlantic ambitions led to the availability of a two-door version, which was arguably more sporting in appearance. It also suited US expectations of a car this size, and in due course the two-door body would go on to have several other applications in the ADO16 range. For the moment, though, it was primarily for North America. Other export territories also took two-door MGs over the years; in 1966–7, for example, there were some for continental European countries and some for Ireland, which actually assembled 264 cars in-territory during 1967.

The interior had its own character, too. Most obvious was a polished wooden dashboard (actually made of Formica on very early cars, but soon changed for real wood veneer). This came with

The MG 1100 was the first of BMC's 'sporty' ADO16s. This early sales brochure traded on the traditional MG slogan – 'Safety Fast'.

Although two-tone paint was one of the MG's unique features, not all MGs had it. This early car with single-tone paint featured in early press photographs.

a Morris-type strip speedometer and its flanking water temperature and fuel gauges, while the toggle switches and ignition keylock were set into it outboard of the steering wheel. There was a

lidded glovebox on the passenger's side, although it was not lockable, and the black-lidded ashtray in the dash centre came with its own internal illumination when the sidelights were on. An internal bonnet release was located below the glovebox – an up-market feature as compared to the external release on the Morris – and all home market cars came with a fresh-air heater.

As for the seats, they were more comfortably padded than those on the Morris, with vertical pleats and leathercloth trim. Real leather could be had at extra cost. The doors contained useful stowage pockets and the passenger cabin was better soundproofed than the Morris – although not so well that the 1100's characteristic gear whine did not intrude at speed. A look in the boot would also have revealed another feature that the Morris lacked – in this case, a trim panel with a wicker-like finish.

As introduced in 1962, the MG 1100 cost £590, but Purchase Tax inflated that by a further £222 5s

The MG was also the first ADO16 to have the twin-carburettor engine. As the picture shows, the MG name was tacked onto the top cover.

3d. Pity the early buyer, because Purchase Tax was cut in November, knocking around £100 off the showroom price, which became £713 9s 7d. For 1963 and 1964 the price remained unchanged, but at the Earls Court show in October 1965 the car was listed at £613 plus £129 5s 5d Purchase Tax, or £742 5s 5d altogether. Though the base price of £613 remained unchanged in 1966, a further adjustment of Purchase Tax had inflated the total cost to £755 4s 0d.

Not many changes were made in those first five years. Thinner front seat backs had arrived with the real wood veneer trim as 1963 opened, to give more legroom in the back. The gear change had been improved in early 1964, as it had on other ADO16s, and larger diameter inlet valves (1.215in instead of 1.155in) arrived at the same time. Later that year the engines took on a positive crankcase ventilation system that had been tried out on US exports of the model from May. For the 1965 model-year came a diaphragm spring clutch, crushable sun visors and a plastic-framed interior mirror, and then May 1966 brought the option of reclining front seats. A heated rear window became a further option later in the year.

The colour choices had remained broadly unchanged, although the need to make the cars attractive to US customers had led to the arrival of some brighter interior options in 1964 and subsequently, and these eventually found their way on to cars for other markets as well. Show cars nevertheless hinted at excesses way beyond reality. At the 1962 Motor Show, the home market four-door in Connaught Green over Old English White with a Dove Grey interior had been accompanied by a 'special exhibit' two-door in Light Coffee over Blue. That never saw production, and nor did the Metallic Lilac Grey with Yellow trim combination on show in 1964. That car, which had left-hand drive, was displayed on a revolving turntable and its doors and bonnet opened and closed as the turntable revolved.

The US versions of the MG 1100 were a special case in many ways. Not only did they have the two-door body shell, but they were marketed with the name of MG Sports Sedan; the significance of the figure 1100 would have been lost in a market that used cubic inches rather than cubic centimetres to describe engine size. They also had laminated windscreens and clear lenses for the front turn

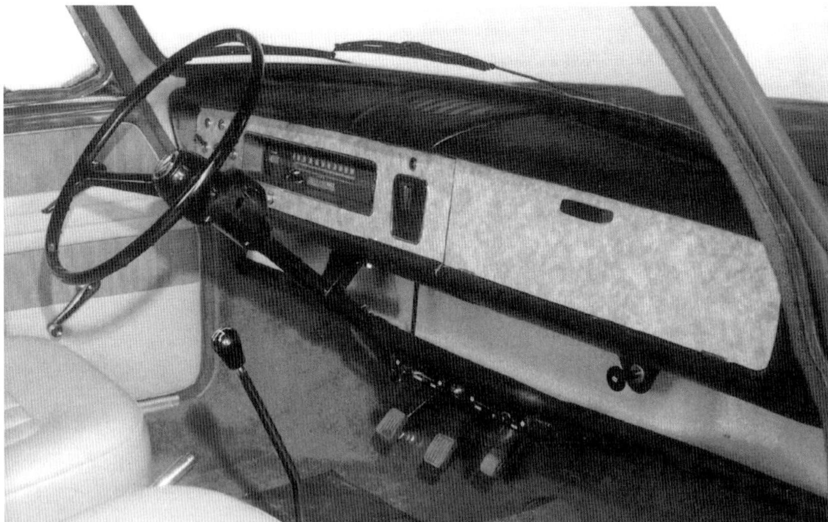

The very early **MG** dashboard was made of Formica with a marbled finish, as seen in this left-hand-drive car. It was not much liked and was replaced by a dashboard with a fake wood veneer, as seen on the right-hand-drive car. Seat had front-to-back pleating, with a separate panel for the thigh roll.

indicators, and no doubt the extra-cost option of whitewall tyres proved popular. A heater cost extra, too.

After the car had been on sale a little over a year, the duotone paint options disappeared from the US catalogues, and then during 1964 the first of some more striking interior options were added. That year a four-door MG Sports Sedan was introduced, too, but the two-doors remained the stronger sellers. Then at the New York Motor Show in April

1965 the US cars took on a new dashboard like that on the home market Austins. Anders Clausager speculates in *MG Saloon Cars* that this was done to make more room for the Normalair air conditioning option that was added to some cars and occupied most of the under-facia parcels shelf.

Early advertising argued that the MG 1100 was 'an MG through and through, offering the same appeal to enthusiasts as the 18/80 did 30 years ago'. Not everybody was convinced, though. Bill Boddy

The 1968 MG models had this short-lived style of seating with transverse pleats. The dashboard still featured a strip speedometer and the original two-spoke steering wheel remained.

of *Motor Sport* famously snorted that 'this MG is like some people, very smooth but lacking in character'. Meanwhile, over in the USA the low gearing that led to rather frenzied noises from under the bonnet prompted *Road & Track* (in January 1963) to argue that the revs needed were 'too many, in the long run, to be entirely healthy. The car sounds good, and feels smooth, even at a steady 75mph, but the fact remains that it is nibbling away at its own innards at a somewhat suicidal rate'.

Over the summer of 1967 the MG joined its stablemates with Riley, Vanden Plas and Wolseley badges in being offered with a more powerful engine. So equipped, it was badged as an MG 1275 and boasted a single-carburettor version of the engine that would arrive as a full-production type later that year in the 1300 model. Only a few hundred were built, as BMC was still tooling up for large volume production of the engine. *Autocar* magazine

described the engine's provenance like this when it tested the 1275cc unit in a Riley-badged ADO16:

> By juggling with components already in production, BMC engine designers have mated the 1275S cylinder block [from the Mini Cooper] with an 1100 transmission, which is unchanged except for a much higher-geared final drive. The [Austin-Healey] Sprite 1275 cylinder head, with its 8.8:1 compression ratio and smaller valves than the Cooper S, is used with the single 1.5in SU carburettor and cast manifolding already on the automatic 1100s. The 1275S cylinder block is inherently much stronger than the 1100 block which it replaces, as the cylinder spacing has been revised, and there is evidence of three years' racing experience in the detail improvements. For example, the pushrod-tappet cover is now cast integral with the block, replacing the original pressed steel cover. The nitrided Cooper S crankshaft is not fitted.

For this larger-capacity engine, buyers had to find an extra £25 on top of the cost of an ordinary 1100, which remained in production. The bigger-engined cars were built between June and October 1967 and had a taller final drive ratio to improve top-end performance. Anders Clausager points out that a US sales leaflet of the period suggested an even taller 3.44:1 final drive was offered there, but doubts whether it was ever fitted in practice.

PRESS VIEWS OF THE MG 1100

Autocar magazine could hardly have been more positive when it reviewed an MG 1100 for its 14 December 1962 issue, despite a number of niggling faults on the test car. These included rattles, a serious steering column vibration, the loss of screws from the glovebox support arm and the total loss of the washer plunger, which disappeared into the dashboard. Yet the car 'performs with such enthusiasm that every minute spent at the wheel becomes a real pleasure … even the most ardent, dyed-in-the-wool MG enthusiast would deem this 1100 a very worthy bearer of the octagon'.

THE MG 1100 IN THE USA

The MG 1100 was always more than a little controversial in the USA. Some owners loved it; others thought it was a dreadful car.

Looking back on the model in its November 1968 issue, *Road Test* magazine noted that 'quality control was awful, the overworked engine flogged itself to pieces more often than not, and the total assembly seemed more haphazard than anyone should expect'. On specifics, they singled out 'the gawdawful interior finish, high noise level and fragile engine mounts among other deficiencies'.

The engine mounts problem was sorted out during the car's lifetime by a production modification, but when the Austin America was introduced as its replacement in spring 1968 (see Chapter 2), a great deal of work had been done to make the car more suitable for US driving conditions.

Ride, roadholding and acceleration were all thought to be of a high order, and there was 'remarkable pulling power from low engine speeds without an accompanying loss of punch at the top end of the rev range'.

The only serious note of dissent was with the padded top of the dashboard, 'which would be better suited to a kitchen dresser'.

On the other side of the Atlantic, *Popular Imported Cars* magazine was similarly impressed by the MG Sports Sedan. 'We have driven the MG Sports Sedan several times over the past few months and can readily see why it is picking up its own coterie of enthusiastic owners,' they wrote in the August 1965 issue. 'We found the handling … actually exciting. Sure-footed as a mountain goat, it feels like a slightly chastened Mini-Cooper.'

The magazine went on to say that 'the feature we liked best … is the uncanny cornering power'. The only real criticism was that 'the MG Sports Sedan is an efficiently designed car, with the cold impersonality normally associated with efficiency, but simply because it crams more space into less overall length than any other model we can think of and still manages to look very much like an automobile instead of a shoebox'.

THE CHANGEOVER PERIOD

October 1967 saw the MG switch to the Mk II ADO16 body shell. The twin-carburettor 1098cc engine remained unchanged for the MG 1100 Mk II, but this model lasted only until March 1968. Buyers were much more interested in the new 1300 version, which at this stage was simply called an MG 1300. Buyers were not to know it yet, but the 'proper' MG 1300 Mk II was just a few months away.

This rather untidy changeover to the new models was partly caused by changes for the US market, and partly too by changes for other markets. The MG 1100 was withdrawn from the US market in autumn 1967 and there was a hiatus in two-door production until the early spring. Anders Clausager says that just five two-door MGs were built between September 1967 and April 1968; the first three went to the USA to fulfil orders.

The next two were examples of the 1300 Mk II that were probably intended for the Geneva Motor Show. It was here that the future of the MG ADO16 became clearer. There were to be no more four-door models, and from April 1968 all the MGs would have two doors – including those for the home market. They would also all have the 1275cc engine, which at this stage had twin HS2 carburettors, double valve springs and 65bhp unless ordered with an automatic transmission, when the single-carburettor 60bhp engine was fitted. An all-synchromesh gearbox would in future be part of the package and – although nobody was saying so yet – there would be more to come later.

The Mk II models lost the two-tone options, but UK cars were now available in both two-door and four-door form. These early Mk IIs are an 1100 four-door and a 1300 two-door, both with perforated wheel discs and side repeater indicators in evidence.

Twin carburettors were in evidence again on the engine of the MG 1300, although the first cars with this engine – known as 1275 models and built over the summer of 1967 – had only a single carburettor. The MG badge is also present, although sharp eyes will spot that it is now a printed sticker and not a metal plate.

The availability of an automatic transmission on the MG had been just one of the changes that accompanied the new body shell in autumn 1967. It could be had on both the 1100 Mk II and the 1300. Both models also gained side repeater flashers on their front wings, new Ambla seats with transverse pleating, recessed interior door handles (a concession to the forthcoming Federal Vehicle Safety Standards in the USA) and a multi-function stalk that operated indicators, horn, headlamp dip and headlamp flasher. There were colour and trim changes, too, though none particularly radical at this stage.

MG 1300 MK II

The definitive MG 1300 Mk II did not arrive until October 1968, when it was displayed at the Earls Court Motor Show. It was available as a two-door only, and the engine had now been further tuned to deliver 70bhp. With the new-found power came a close-ratio gearbox, with taller first, second and third gears to make the most of the extended rev range. An automatic option was still listed, and this time there was no reduction in engine power: the automatics had the same 70bhp twin-carburettor engine as the manuals.

From autumn 1968 the Mk II MG dashboard was a little more sporting, with the round dials pioneered on Riley models and an attractive three-spoke steering wheel. Seat pleating now ran over the edges of the cushions.

Prices were listed in the Motor Show catalogue as £845 8s 4d (£660 plus Purchase Tax) for the manual car, and £941 5s 0d (£735 plus Purchase Tax) for the automatic.

The new cars came in a range of colours that was largely new and no longer included the two-tone options that were increasingly being seen as old-fashioned. They also came with radial tyres as standard, original equipment being Dunlop SP68s, and the wheel discs had the new perforated style common to all the Mk II ADO16 models. Otherwise, exterior changes were limited to a modified boot handle that now incorporated the number-plate light.

There were changes inside the passenger cabin, too. The front door pockets had gone, along with the cubby-boxes in the rear doors. The upholstery — unique to the MG models — was in Ambla, once again with longitudinal pleats but now with a centre rear armrest as well. The dashboard, meanwhile, had changed completely, and now had the three circular dials of the Riley 1300 and the new 1300GT models from the Austin and Morris marques. Rocker switches had their functions clearly marked, and there was a more sporty-looking steering wheel, now smaller with a diameter of 16 inches, a padded rim trimmed in leather and three perforated alloy spokes. Unfortunately, its angle had not been

changed, so the sporty appearance was not quite backed up by the driving experience.

There were no longer any MGs for North America. These were changing times, and the model shipped across the Atlantic was now the Austin America (see Chapter 2). The changing times required more regular product refreshment, and so there would be new ranges of colours for both the 1970 and 1971 model-years, the 1970 changes arriving with the 1969 Motor Show that autumn, but the 1971 changes being delayed until February 1971.

In the meantime, the automatic gearbox option had been discontinued in 1969. The 1970 cars gained the engine splash shield that was applied across the ADO16 range that year, and at the end of 1970 a steering lock became standard (after being fitted to some export cars for some time) and front-seat safety belts became a line-fit option instead of a dealer-fit option.

The end of MG production came in September 1971, but that was not quite the end of MG badges on an ADO16 derivative. The Cowley plant continued to build CKD kits until 1973, and in that year Authi in Spain built a pair of prototypes of what they called the MG Victoria. There is more about these cars in Chapter 6, but they were not followed by production examples.

PAINT AND TRIM COLOURS

MG 1100 Mk I (1962–7)

Body	Interior
Black	Black, Cherokee Red, Dove Grey, Green or Terra Cotta
British Racing Green	Cherokee Red
Connaught Green	Black, Dove Grey or Green
Old English White	Black, Cherokee Red or Terra Cotta
Smoke Grey	Reef Blue
Tartan Red	Dove Grey or Black
Connaught Green over Old English White	Dove Grey or Green
Old English White over Sandy Beige	Black, Cherokee Red or Terra Cotta
Smoke Grey over Old English White	Reef Blue

Black was a special-order colour.

British Racing Green was a non-standard colour used on only a few cars during 1966.

The initial trim colours were Dove Grey, Reef Blue and Terra Cotta; Green became available from early 1966. Terra Cotta was discontinued in spring 1966. Cherokee Red trim became available on non-US cars during 1964, and Black during 1966.

MG Sports Sedan (1963–4 model-years)

Body	Interior
Black	Black, Cherokee Red, Dove Grey, or Terra Cotta
Connaught Green	Dove Grey
Old English White	Black, Cherokee Red or Terra Cotta
Tartan Red	Dove Grey or Black
Smoke Grey	Reef Blue
Connaught Green over Old English White	Dove Grey
Old English White over Sandy Beige	Cherokee Red or Terra Cotta
Smoke Grey over Old English White	Reef Blue

The two-tone options were discontinued for the 1964 model-year, but the other options remained unchanged.

MG Sports Sedan (1965–7 model-years)

Body	Interior
Black	Cherokee Red
Connaught Green	Black or Green
Old English White	Black
Smoke Grey	Reef Blue
Tartan Red	Black

MG 1100 Mk II and 1300 (1968 model-year)

Body	Interior
Black	Black, Cherokee Red or Green
Smoke Grey	Reef Blue
Snowberry White	Black or Cherokee Red
Tartan Red	Black
Connaught Green over Snowberry White	Green
Smoke Grey over Snowberry White	Reef Blue
Snowberry White over Sandy Beige	Black or Cherokee Red

Black was a special-order colour.

MG 1300 (1969 model-year)

Body	Interior
Bermuda Blue	Black
Connaught Green	Black or Mushroom
Cumulus Grey	Galleon Blue
Fawn Brown	Mushroom
Pale Primrose Yellow	Black
Sandy Beige	Mushroom
Snowberry White	Black or Icon Red
Tartan Red	Black
Trafalgar Blue	Galleon Blue

Pale Primrose Yellow was available for export only.

MG 1300 (1970 model-year)

Body	Interior
Antelope	Autumn Leaf or Black
Bermuda Blue	Black
Blue Royale	Galleon Blue
Bronze Yellow	Black
Connaught Green	Autumn Leaf
Cumulus Grey	Galleon Blue
Fawn Brown	Autumn Leaf
Flame Red	Black
Glacier White	Black or Icon Red

Bronze Yellow was available for export only.

MG 1300 (1971 model-year)
These changes actually took effect from February 1971.

Body	Interior
Bedouin	Autumn Leaf
Damask Red	Navy
Flame Red	Navy
Glacier White	Geranium or Navy
Limeflower	Limeflower or Navy
Midnight Blue	Geranium or Navy
Racing Green	Limeflower
Wild Moss	Olive

MG 1100 AND 1300 IDENTIFICATION NUMBERS

Car numbers ('chassis' or VIN numbers)

G GS1	Mk I four-door	
G G2S 1	Mk I two-door	
G A2S3	Mk I two-door	
G A2S4	Mk II and Mk III two-door (1100 and 1300)	
G A2S5	Mk II and Mk III two-door (1100 and 1300)	
G AS3	Mk II and Mk III four-door (1100 and 1300)	
G AS4	Mk II and Mk III four-door (1100 and 1300)	
G2S1	Mk I two-door	from 6710
G2S	Mk II and Mk III 1100 and 1300, two-door	from 9100
GA2S	Mk II and Mk III 1100 and 1300, two-door, for USA	from 9100
GS	1100 and 1300 Mk II and Mk III, four-door	from 86300

These prefix codes are followed by an L for LHD models and then by the serial number. The serial number is followed by an A (Longbridge assembly) or an M (Cowley assembly). A full number might therefore read G A2S3L 56789 A.

These prefix codes are followed by the serial number, which in turn is followed by the letter P. A full number might therefore read G2S 9111 P.

Commission numbers

G 16 S	Mk I four-door, Cowley build	from 6292
G 16 S	Mk II 1100, Mk I and Mk II 1300 four-door	from 89153
G 16 2S	Mk I two-door, Cowley build	from 6946
G 16 2S	1300, two-door, Cowley build	from 26875
G 16 2S	1300 Mk II, two-door	from 32579

These prefix codes are followed by the serial number, which in turn is followed by an M (Cowley assembly). A full number might therefore read G 16S-6011 M.

Body shell numbers

SCB	Mk I two-door	from 101
GA2S	Mk I two-door for USA	from 101

Engine codes

10GR	1100 Mk I
12G, 12H	1275 Mk I
10H	1100 Mk II
12H	1300 Mk II and Mk III

On Mk I models, the engine prefix code is followed by a transmission type code and an H (High compression) or an L (Low compression). The final segment of an engine number is then the serial number, so that a full number might read 10GR-TAH54321. The most common transmission type codes were SA (close-ratio manual gearbox), TA (standard-ratio manual gearbox) and A (automatic gearbox).

On Mk II and Mk III models, the engine prefix code is followed by a four-digit code consisting of three numbers and a letter. Typical would be 199C, which indicates twin carburettors, a 22-amp dynamo, crankcase ventilation and close-ratio gearbox. The H or L code then prefixes the serial number, so that a typical number might be 10H199C-H56789.

hard top–soft ride
thanks to Hydrolastic® suspension

The 1930's were hard times on the road, as elsewhere. The M.G. 18/80 met the demand of enthusiasts for first-class performance and road holding, but it was hard going—literally. Today's descendant the M.G. 1100, with the fabulous fluid suspension and front wheel drive hugs the road even better, but you never notice the bumps. In fact it's an M.G. through and through offering the same appeal to enthusiasts as the 18/80 did 30 years ago. You don't believe it? Then try one today and let it prove itself.

Safety Fast **MG 1100** *£590 + £123.9.7 PT 4 door de-luxe*

BMC are the World's largest Manufacturers of front wheel drive vehicles. Over 1,000,000 have been produced.

Marketing of the MG models always drew heavily on the traditions of the brand. This 1964 advertisement for the MG 1100 was typical.

'The most exciting thing that ever happened to family motoring' claimed this 1966 advertisement of the ADO16; add an **MG** badge, and you apparently had it all.

MG 1100 AND 1300 PRODUCTION

These production figures are for calendar-years, and were provided by the manufacturer during its time as the Austin Rover Group.

Year	Home	Export	Total	
1962	0	4,577	4,577	(2-door)
	2,561	740	3,301	(4-door)
1963	1	8,062	8,063	(2-door)
	11,649	6,692	18,341	(4-door)
1964	0	4,946	4,946	(2-door)
	15,503	12,254	27,757	(4-door)
1965	0	3,776	3,776	(2-door)
	14,423	9,804	24,227	(4-door)
1966	1	4,333	4,334	(2-door)
	12,607	5,336	17,943	(4-door)
1967	3,744	3,053	6,797	(1100)
	927	392	1,319	(1300)
1968	233	565	798	(1100)
	8,395	2,584	10,979	(1300)
1969	3,838	4,424	8,262	
1970	2,224	1,417	3,641	
1971	2,472	3,068	5,540	
1972	0	1,680	1,680	
1973	0	1,128	1,128	

The 1967 figures include a few hundred MG 1275 models, of which some were for the home market and others for export. The export figures for 1967 also include 264 cars for Ireland.

The 1972 export figure of 1,680 MG 1300s is thought to have been a CKD order for Spain.

RILEY KESTREL

The second sporting marque in the BMC line-up was Riley, an independent company until it was absorbed into the Nuffield combine in 1940. In effect a more junior member of the BMC combine than MG, despite its illustrious past, Riley had continued to exist mainly to keep long-standing Riley dealers and their customers happy. Though memories of the Riley marque's heyday lingered into the 1960s, nobody was in any doubt that there had been no more real Rileys after the last Riley-designed car to wear the blue diamond badge was phased out in 1955.

Perhaps that sounds more cynical than it needs to. After all, the Riley One-Point-Five that the Riley-badged ADO16 was to replace was actually a rather good car, with decent performance from its 1.5-litre engine and more than a touch of style about its modified Morris Minor body shell. But what really upset devotees of the blue diamond in 1965 was BMC's decision to revive a much-loved name from Riley's past and call the new front-wheel-drive car a Riley Kestrel.

That was the name applied to the car when it was announced at the Earls Court Motor Show in October 1965, at the same time as the Wolseley 1100 with which it shared much of its specification. Rileys were distinguished by a traditional Riley grille in a unique front panel, with horizontal sidelight-and-indicator units in dummy grilles on either side. There were blue diamond badges on the hubcaps and perforated embellisher rings to cover the rest of the wheels. The flanks carried full-length bright metal strips like those on the MG 1100, although the colour division on the Riley did not use these as a dividing line. Instead, the upper colour was applied to roof and roof pillars, as on the Vanden Plas models. The boot lid was adorned with a chrome strip and the Riley Kestrel name in bright metal script, and the number-plate light was mounted on the bumper, as on the Vanden Plas 1100.

All the Kestrels had four-door bodies. On the inside, the expectations of Riley customers were met with leather upholstery that featured horizontal pleats, and an American walnut dashboard veneer. Invisibly, the cars had more sound-deadening than most of their stablemates in the ADO16 range. The door cards were all neatly pleated, and the front doors carried useful oddments bins. Best of all was the dashboard layout, with three circular dials – speedometer, rev counter and multi-instrument dial covering fuel, water temperature and oil pressure. This arrangement made the Riley the only 1100 to have a rev counter, which was something that many MG owners missed in their 1100s.

Like the **MG**, the Riley could be had with two-tone paint schemes, but the colour split was different. The Riley grille made this one of the more attractive ADO16 variants.

The Riley always had its own bonnet, with a 'peak' at the front to suit the special grille. This is on a Mk II model and shows the metal Riley emblem that sat on the peak.

Most important was the choice of engine, for the Riley needed the best performance available. The best available in 1965 was the twin-carburettor 1098cc unit, exactly as fitted to the MG, Wolseley and Vanden Plas models, boasting all of 55bhp and now (from October 1965) fitted with positive crank-case ventilation. Only the four-speed manual gear-box, initially with no synchromesh on first gear, was available. So the Riley did have to rely on its cosmetic features to distinguish it from the other upmarket models of the ADO16 family. Fortunately, the Riley front end and two-tone colour schemes (available at no extra cost) did suit the car rather well. BMC positioned it above the MG in the range, with an initial asking price of £780 18s 9d (the base price was £645, the rest Purchase Tax) in October 1965.

Single-colour cars were available too, of course. This was an early example, and shows the special hubcaps with their unique Riley blue diamond badges. BMC's view was that it always helped to have a couple of pretty girls in the photograph.

Why do Riley owners look so dashed superior?

Test-drive the new twin-carb. Riley Kestrel—and you'll find out

See why the Kestrel's the world's most compact, most luxurious sporting five-seater. Note the real-leather luxury, the rich gleam of natural wood, the door-to-door welcome of deep-pile carpets. Here's space and comfort that only an east-west engine and Hydrolastic ® suspension can give you. Here's twin-carburetter performance and disc-brake safety and the kind of road-holding you get only with front-wheel drive.

Are you the sporty Kestrel type?

Would you care to join the club? Then see your Riley dealer. The Kestrel is £780 18s. 9d., including £135 18s. 9d. P.T. The test-drive is free. And the footman can be hired.

R53

Although the Riley Kestrel was mechanically the same as the MG 1100, its marketing was different. This time, the emphasis was on the perceived superiority of the old-established brand. The advertisement is from 1965, when the Kestrel was new.

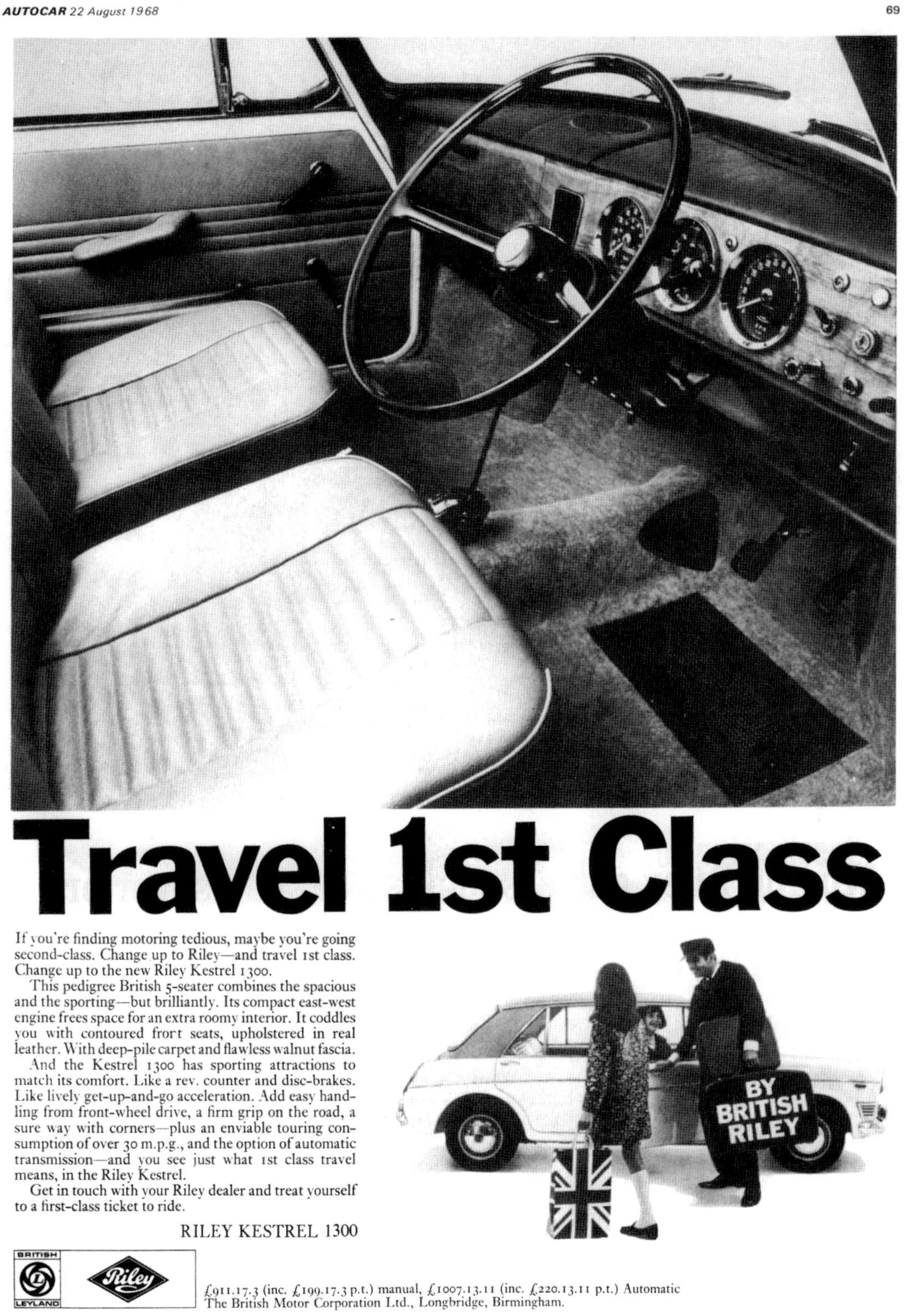

Travel 1st Class

If you're finding motoring tedious, maybe you're going second-class. Change up to Riley—and travel 1st class. Change up to the new Riley Kestrel 1300.

This pedigree British 5-seater combines the spacious and the sporting—but brilliantly. Its compact east-west engine frees space for an extra roomy interior. It coddles you with contoured front seats, upholstered in real leather. With deep-pile carpet and flawless walnut fascia.

And the Kestrel 1300 has sporting attractions to match its comfort. Like a rev. counter and disc-brakes. Like lively get-up-and-go acceleration. Add easy handling from front-wheel drive, a firm grip on the road, a sure way with corners—plus an enviable touring consumption of over 30 m.p.g., and the option of automatic transmission—and you see just what 1st class travel means, in the Riley Kestrel.

Get in touch with your Riley dealer and treat yourself to a first-class ticket to ride.

RILEY KESTREL 1300

£911.17.3 (inc. £199.17.3 p.t.) manual, £1007.13.11 (inc. £220.13.11 p.t.) Automatic
The British Motor Corporation Ltd., Longbridge, Birmingham.

Superiority again characterized Riley advertising, which in this case was for the new 1300 version of the Kestrel in 1968. It would not be long before the Kestrel name was dropped ... and then the Riley name went altogether.

The Kestrel had its own dashboard, with three round dials against a wood-veneer background. The steering-wheel centre, of course, carried the blue diamond badge.

This is the Riley version of the 1100 engine – identical in every respect to the MG version but, of course, with a Riley identification plate.

The Kestrel never sold anything like as well as the cheaper MG 1100, and export sales were always low because the Riley name meant little outside the UK. A running change was made in May 1966 when reclining front seats became a £15 option, but the Kestrel was never offered with an automatic gearbox. At this stage, at least, it was probably not thought to suit the sporting Riley image.

'Make no mistake, the Riley Kestrel *is* just another 1100, inheriting all the model's virtues and faults,' said *Motor* in its 9 October 1965 road test. 'We sympathise with those people who had hoped for a bigger A-series engine.' Comfort and handling came in for the usual praise, but the car was still noisy: 'Better sound-proofing makes the Kestrel quieter than the cheaper 1100s but the engine and transmission can still be heard humming away up to 70mph when the noise mingles, indistinguishably, with modest wind and tyre roar … there is still an unpleasant engine resonance between 67–70mph –

Still recognizably a Riley thanks to its grille, the car was gradually succumbing to the BMC corporate plan by the time of the Mk II models. There were still distinctive Riley hubcaps, now on the universal perforated wheel discs. Publicity pictures were usually of single-tone cars, and the two-toning on this example does not really do it any favours.

A publicity photograph like this could only have been taken in the 1960s! Sadly, the Kestrel 1100 is another single-tone car; it was almost as if the Riley people were apologetic about their good-looking two-tone options.

another irritation that has been evident since the first 1100s were made.'

Over the summer of 1967, Rileys became available with the 1275cc single-carburettor engine that was also introduced for MG, Wolseley and Vanden Plas derivatives. These cars, badged as Riley 1275 derivatives, cost an extra £25 and were made available in small numbers alongside the existing 1098cc models. *Autocar* magazine was able to test one in its issue of 8 June 1967, and certainly liked the new engine:

The most significant improvements were in the 1275's obvious ruggedness, and relaxed 'feel', rather than in actual acceleration. The 1275 engined 1100 is now the highest geared of all the small transverse engined BMC cars, and felt much more relaxed at any road speed. There was a useful reduction in the tiresome transmission whines that have afflicted Minis and 1100s for years.

Yet the Kestrel still fell short in some areas and, unforgivably for a car with sporting pretensions, one of those was the brakes. 'The Kestrel could … benefit from improved brakes', complained *Autocar*: 'The pedal "feel" itself is poor, as the system feels characteristically spongy and lacks precision. When used hard the brakes fade much earlier than expected; they became uncertain and smoked well before the end of our rigorous fade test, when many other cars would not have faltered.'

The *Autocar* test quoted the final drive on this car as having a 3.65:1 ratio, and that ratio certainly did become standard on all 1275cc-engined derivatives of the ADO16. However, the very early 'transitional' 1275 models had a taller 3.44:1 final drive, which was discontinued after an unknown quantity of cars had been built.

MK II RILEYS

Like its MG counterpart, the Riley suffered from a rather untidy transition to a new model between 1967 and 1968. Between October 1967 and October 1968 there were Kestrel 1100 Mk II models and Kestrel 1300 models, and only from October 1968 did the Riley 1300 Mk II become available, having lost the Kestrel name in the process. Riley enthusiasts like to think that their objections to the use

This is one of the last Kestrels; Rileys would become plain 1300s during the 1969 model-year, which was their last.

There was still a twin-carburettor engine under the bonnet, and it still bore a Riley label. This is a Riley 1300 Mk II.

The Mk II cars had a 1300 badge above the plinth on the boot lid, which was still fluted, and they carried the Riley name with a 'Mk II' badge.

of the name were a factor in its demise. All of these cars could be had with automatic transmission for an extra cost of £75, and all of them had the Mk II body shell with its shortened rear wing projections, whether or not they carried the Mk II name.

Like its MG stablemate, the Riley became a 1300 Mk II for the 1969 model-year. New colours arrived and the old two-tone options disappeared altogether. Like the MG, the Riley 1300 also had a close-ratio all-synchromesh gearbox, and radial tyres were standard equipment. On the outside, these cars were readily recognizable by the blue British Leyland badge on their left-hand front wings; the right-hand wing did not have one, as was the case on most BL cars of the time. Wheel discs were, of course, the new perforated type. The steering wheel rim was

now trimmed in leather and an MG-type fluted boot handle was now fitted, incorporating the number-plate light so that this now disappeared from the bumper. Leather contact surfaces were still a feature of the upholstery. Production had also been transferred from Longbridge to Cowley.

Prices had started to creep up. The last of the Mk I cars had been priced at £672 before Purchase

PAINT AND TRIM COLOURS

The two-tone paint schemes were a no-cost option for the Riley models.

Riley Kestrel (1962–7)

Body	Interior
Agate Red	Cherokee Red
Aquamarine	Horizon Blue
Black	Cherokee Red or Green
Cumberland Green	Green
Sandy Beige	Mushroom
Snowberry White	Cherokee Red
Arianca Beige over Sandy Beige	Mushroom
Cumberland Green over Snowberry White	Green
Sandy Beige over Snowberry White	Mushroom
Snowberry White over Aquamarine	Horizon Blue
Sandy Beige over Fawn Brown	Mushroom

Riley 1300 Mk II

Body	Interior
Bermuda Blue	Black
Connaught Green	Black
Cumulus Grey	Galleon Blue
Damask Red	Icon Red
Fawn Brown	Mushroom
Sandy Beige	Mushroom
Snowberry White	Black
Trafalgar Blue	Galleon Blue

RILEY KESTREL AND 1300 IDENTIFICATION NUMBERS

Car numbers ('chassis' or VIN numbers)

R AS1	Kestrel 1100	serials 101 to 12223
R AS4	Kestrel 1275	from 12224
R AS4	1100 Mk II	(final car) 16714
R A4S5	1300	from 16715
R A4S5	1300 Mk II	(final car) 21629

These prefix codes are followed by an L on LHD models and then by the serial number. The serial number may be followed by an M (Cowley assembly). A full number might therefore read R AS4L 12345 M.

Commission numbers

R 16 S	Kestrel, Longbridge build	from 101
R 16 S	1300	from 1582
R 16 S	1300 Mk II, Cowley build	from 5949

These prefix codes are followed by the serial number, which in turn is followed by an L (Longbridge assembly) or an M (Cowley assembly). A full number might therefore read R 16S-5999 M.

Body shell numbers

| RS | Kestrel | from 101 |
| RS | Kestrel and 1300 | from 1600 |

These prefix codes are followed by the serial number, which in turn is followed by the letter L or P, which both indicate Longbridge build. A full number might therefore read RS 2111 P.

Engine codes

10R	Kestrel (1100)
12G, 12H	1275
10H	1100 Mk II
12H	1300 Mk II

On Kestrels, the engine prefix code is followed by a transmission type code and an H (High compression) or an L (Low compression). The final segment of an engine number is then the serial number, so that a full number might read 10R-SAH55443. The most common transmission type codes were SA (close-ratio manual gearbox), TA (standard-ratio manual gearbox) and A (automatic gearbox).

On 1300 models the engine prefix code is followed by a four-digit code consisting of three numbers and a letter. Typical would be 199C, which indicates twin carburettors, a 22-amp dynamo, crankcase ventilation and close-ratio gearbox. The H or L code then prefixes the serial number, so that a typical number might be 10H199C-H66778.

RILEY KESTREL AND 1300 PRODUCTION

These production figures are for calendar-years, and were provided by the manufacturer during its time as the Austin Rover Group. The 1967 figures include the Riley 1275 models.

Year	Home	Export	Total	
1965	3,601	212	3,813	
1966	5,147	706	5,853	
1967	2,236	366	2,602	(1100)
	897	36	933	(1300)
1968	24	60	84	(1100)
	4,801	231	5,032	(1300)
1969	2,874	284	3,158	
	19,580	1895	21,475	

Tax, and a further £20 was added to that for the short-lived 1275 models. This new higher price then remained in place for the 1100 Mk II models. The first 1300s had a base cost of £712, and then the 1969-model 1300 Mk IIs cost £730.

By this stage, however, the writing on the wall was very clear indeed. The Riley 1300 was the slowest-selling ADO16 saloon during the 1969 model-year, and it did not offer much that could not be had from the cheaper MG model or indeed from the new 1300GT saloons that wore Austin and Morris badges. Besides, the sales of all Riley models now accounted for only a tiny proportion of the cars that the marque's owners at British Leyland were selling. In business terms, Riley no longer made sense, and in the summer of 1969 the inevitable happened. 'British Leyland will stop making Riley cars from today', read a press release dated 9 July. 'With less than 1 per cent of the home market, they are not viable.'

Technical Specifications, MG and Riley ADO16 saloons

Engine
1100 models
BMC A-series 4-cylinder, with iron block and cylinder head
1098cc (64.58 × 83.72mm)
Overhead valves; chain-driven camshaft
Three-bearing crankshaft
Compression ratio 8.9:1 (8.2:1 available for export)
Two SU HS2 1.25in carburettors
55bhp at 5,500rpm
61 lb ft at 2,500rpm

1275 models
BMC A-series 4-cylinder, with iron block and cylinder head
1275cc (70.6 × 81.28mm)
Overhead valves; chain-driven camshaft
Three-bearing crankshaft
Compression ratio 8.8:1
One SU HS4 1.5in carburettor
58bhp at 5,250rpm
69 lb ft at 3,000rpm

1300 models
BMC A-series 4-cylinder, with iron block and cylinder head
1275cc (70.6 × 81.28mm)
Overhead valves; chain-driven camshaft
Three-bearing crankshaft
Compression ratio 9.75:1
Two SU HS2 carburettors
65bhp at 5,750rpm
70bhp at 6,000rpm for Mk II models
71 lb ft at 3,000rpm
77 lb ft at 3,000rpm for Mk II models

Transmission
Four-speed manual gearbox, with no synchromesh on
first gear with synchromesh on all forward gears from
mid-1968
Gear ratios   (1100): 3.63:1, 2.17:1, 1.41:1, 1.00:1,
        reverse 3.63:1
        (1275 and 1300): 3.52:1, 2.22:1, 1.43:1,
        1.00:1, reverse 3.54:1
Four-speed AP automatic gearbox optional from
autumn 1967 to summer 1969 on MG models; available
from 1968 on Riley models; gear ratios 2.69:1, 1.85:1,
1.46:1, 1.00:1, reverse 2.69
Front-wheel drive

Axle ratio
1100: 4.13:1
1275: 3.44:1 (early models); 3.65:1 (late models)
1300: 3.65:1
1300 automatic: 3.76:1

Suspension, steering and brakes
All-round independent suspension with Hydrolastic
units, interconnected front to rear. Front suspension
with wishbones; rear suspension with trailing arms and
anti-roll bar
Rack-and-pinion steering
Front disc brakes and rear drum brakes

Dimensions

Overall length	12ft 2.7in (3,726mm)
Overall width	5ft 0.4in (1534mm)
Overall height	4ft 4.7in (1,338mm)
Wheelbase	7ft 9.5in (2,375mm)
Front track	4ft 3.5in (1,308mm)
Rear track	4ft 2.9in (1,292mm)

Wheels and tyres
12-inch steel disc wheels, with 4-inch rims
5.50 × 12 cross-ply tyres
145 × 12 radial tyres (available from 1968)

Unladen weights

MG 1100	1,820lb (825kg) approx
Riley Kestrel	1,850lb (839kg) approx

Performance and fuel
MG 1100

0–60mph	18.4 sec
Maximum	85mph (136.8km/h)
Fuel consumption	29mpg (9.76ltr/100km)

MG 1275

0–60mph	17.3 sec
Maximum	88mph (141.6km/h)
Fuel consumption	30mpg (9.43ltr/100km)

Riley 1300 Mk II

0–60mph	14.1 sec
Maximum	93mph (149.7km/h)
Fuel consumption	27mpg (10.48ltr/100km)

CHAPTER SIX

WOLSELEY AND VANDEN PLAS: THE LUXURY MODELS

The luxury marque of the old Nuffield Organisation in pre-BMC days had been Wolseley, and although it had become no more than a badge under BMC, it still retained the image of quality appointments and discreet sophistication. Many of the old Wolseley dealers were still in business, too, and BMC needed to keep them happy as it pressed ahead with its new model ranges for the 1960s. So from a very early stage, a Wolseley version of the ADO16 was on the cards. Like the Riley Kestrel, however, it was put on hold while the old Wolseley 1500 (another Morris Minor derivative) remained in production.

In the mean time, ADO16's potential as the basis of a compact luxury car had not escaped notice elsewhere. In particular, the possibilities had occurred to Fred Connolly, head of the Connolly leather company that supplied much of Britain's motor industry. Mr Connolly decided that he wanted such a car for his own personal use, and so during 1962 he persuaded the coachbuilding specialists at the Vanden Plas company in Kingsbury, north London, to convert a Morris 1100 to his specification.

The car was painted in two-tone dark green and Sherwood Green, and had a Champagne beige interior. The seats were trimmed in leather, there was polished wood trim in typical Vanden Plas fashion, and for good measure there was a special, enlarged grille. The car retained its Morris badges, but it attracted the attention of senior management within BMC, which owned Vanden Plas by this stage and used the company to trim upmarket versions of Austin models.

So it was that the car appeared on the Vanden Plas stand at the 1963 Earls Court Motor Show,

The first Vanden Plas ADO16 was really a private commission and had some differences from the eventual production cars. One of them was the grille, which at this stage was not intended to carry the Vanden Plas family look.

next to examples of the Princess 3-litre and 4-litre luxury saloons. By this stage it had been given a new front end with a grille and inset auxiliary lamps in the mould of those on the existing Vanden Plas saloons. It also had a twin-carburettor engine, a radio and a heated rear window, and there was a sliding roof as well, which may have been in Fred Connolly's original specification. The show catalogue also gave a price: £740 basic, plus £154 14s 7d Purchase Tax, making a total cost of £894 14s 7d.

Some sources suggest that no proper production plan then existed, and that the car was shown largely to gauge public reaction. That may or may not be true: what is clear is that Vanden Plas had

DEV 1 – Development Car no 1 – was the prototype of the production cars and was constructed at the Vanden Plas works in Kingsbury.

already started work on a production prototype and that the first examples of the new model were delivered to customers over the winter of 1963–4. In fact, customers flocked to buy it.

BMC pedalled hard to keep up. There was no way that demand could be met by the Vanden Plas works at Kingsbury, and so production was arranged to take place on the Longbridge lines. Even though all the cars had a Vanden Plas commission number and a Vanden Plas Job Card, only a handful of development cars seem to have been completed at Kingsbury, a fact that BMC did not rush to make public. Anders Clausager (in his *Complete Catalogue of Austin Cars since 1945*) notes that the first three years' worth of production was done entirely at Longbridge. Their sliding sunroofs (a feature not found on any other ADO16 derivative) were added to the body shells by Weathershields, a specialist in such installations who were based at Bishop Street in Birmingham's Digbeth district.

VANDEN PLAS 1100

The Vanden Plas 1100 was considerably more expensive than other ADO16s. Its showroom price of nearly £900 has to be compared with those of the basic Morris 1100 (£610 15s 5d in De Luxe form) and the MG 1100 (£713 9s 7d). For £900,

a British buyer in late 1962 could have bought an Austin A60 Countryman, a Ford Zephyr Six saloon, an MG Magnette, a Singer Vogue estate, a Sunbeam Rapier sports saloon or a Vauxhall Velox saloon – and in every case would have walked away with some change. Yet there was nothing quite like the Vanden Plas 1100, which had a unique combination of small-car economy with a spacious interior and a luxurious ambience.

The special features began on the outside, with that characteristic Vanden Plas grille surmounted by a red crown and flanked by inset fog and spot lamps. Horizontal sidelight and turn signal units made the car look wider, while over-riders from the 1100 De Luxe added to the 'big-car' appearance. The chrome hubcaps were distinctive, too, with embellishers and the VP symbol on black centre finishers. Then there were distinctive paint schemes, all discreet and many of them two-tone, and all with a hand-painted gold coachline down each of the car's flanks. The fuel filler – chromed, of course – was lockable.

At the rear, the bumper wrapped around the sides of the car more than on other 1100s, and substantial over-riders directly under the tail-light clusters matched those at the front. The number-plate lights were concealed under a plinth on the bumper, and there was a horizontal strip of chrome

Greys, blacks, browns and dark greens were typical Vanden Plas colours, and they did help to give the cars a unique kind of dignity.

above the number-plate, which doubled as embellisher and boot handle. Finally, the Vanden Plas name appeared as a script badge on the left of the boot lid, matched on the right by the model-name of Princess 1100.

It was a thoroughly attractive package, and not at all reminiscent of the more cynical badge-engineering to which BMC was becoming increasingly prone. The promise of the exterior was fulfilled inside the passenger cabin, too, where there was full Connolly leather upholstery, with individual folding armrests for each reclining front seat and a centre armrest for the rear bench. The dashboard was a full-width swathe of polished walnut, with a pair of traditional round dials recessed into it and an eyeball air vent at each end; a black 'switch panel' outboard of the driver added a distinguished touch.

Walnut door cappings matched the wood of the dash, while the backs of the front seats carried folding walnut picnic tables. The suspended headlining was in West of England cloth, no less, while the carpets were Wilton. Each rear quarter-panel contained a reading light, and extra touches included a dashboard clock (by Smiths or by Jaeger – BMC believed in dual-sourcing), a cigar lighter, a special chromed ashtray in the rear, and an electric screenwash. Even the boot carpet was properly bound at its edges.

By the time of the 1964 Motor Show, the Purchase Tax had been recalculated and the total price had gone up to £895 14s 7d, although the basic cost of £740 was unchanged. A year later, the Earls Court Show catalogue quoted a basic price of £765 with Purchase Tax of £160 18s 9d, making the total figure now £925 18s 9d. At the 1966 Show it was £765 plus Purchase Tax of £177 0s 8d (total £942 0s 8d) – and a year after that the car was replaced by the inevitably more expensive 1300-engined version. Well over 14,000 had been sold by then, and the car had attracted export customers as well as those on the home market. Sales had slowed in 1967, however: the new and cheaper Wolseley 1100 had arrived in October 1965 and had probably been making inroads into Vanden Plas sales.

In fact, BMC had stumbled upon a market niche in which the Vanden Plas 1100 was inadvertently a pioneer. The car had a strong appeal to well-off retirees, who perhaps had been used to a larger luxury saloon such as a Humber, Rover or one of the bigger Vanden Plas models during their working lives. Downsizing to a smaller and more affordable car need not now mean losing the creature comforts that those larger cars afforded. The 1100 – available only with four doors so that less agile friends could use the back seats with reasonable ease – fitted the bill admirably.

Oddly, though, BMC advertising for the Vanden Plas seemed to miss this point altogether. Most advertisements promoted the 1100 as a woman's car: 'Today's smart car is a Vanden Plas' read one of them, suggesting a fashionable appeal. The truth was that the car was far too expensive for the majority of women drivers, who in the early 1960s typically drove a second car bought by their husbands. Only a lucky few would have been able to afford a Vanden Plas 1100.

None of that prevented BMC and Vanden Plas looking at ways of exploiting the Vanden Plas 1100 concept. Two Princess Countryman prototypes were built for evaluation, but no Vanden Plas estate car ever entered production. There was even an attempt to sell the Vanden Plas 1100 in the USA, where it was marketed as an MG Princess (because the Vanden Plas name was almost unknown on the far side of the Atlantic). The cars were essentially left-hand-drive versions of the standard article, with MG badges on their grilles, boot lids, hubcaps and steering wheel bosses. Built between 1964 and September 1966, the cars sold there alongside the MG Sports Sedan, which was the US version of the MG 1100. They were nevertheless not a success, and just 154 had been built when production was brought to an end.

Motor tested a Vanden Plas Princess 1100 in its issue dated 31 October 1964 and described it as 'the first major attempt to sophisticate a small car … there is probably no other production car in the world that combines so much luxury with a touring consumption of nearly 40mpg.'

This version of the ADO16 was much quieter than others, and 'heavy sound damping has minimised the noise level which at a cruising speed of

The Vanden Plas 1100 was quite a hit in some of BMC's overseas markets, even though – or perhaps because – it was peculiarly British in inspiration. This publicity picture, issued in the UK, showed a left-hand-drive car for Switzerland.

75mph is indistinguishable from the low overall rumble of wind and tyre roar'. As for the luxury interior, 'The large comfortable front seats are all that one expects of a luxury car … [but] … compared with other BMC 1100s, the thickness of the reclining backrests steals considerable legroom from rear-seat passengers and four tall people might find the accommodation cramped.'

Despite Vanden Plas's best efforts, 'the mass-production ancestry can still be seen in various small details like doors without zero-torque locks that need a hefty slam to shut and front quarter-lights which are imperfectly sealed when shut'. Those efforts had made a big difference to the price, too: 'costing £300 more than the Austin/Morris 1100s, and £200 more than the MG, the baby Princess is by no means cheap at £896 and its performance is modest for the price. But if speed and great size are not important this is a delightful car … Even so, better performance would broaden the appeal of this opulent little car.'

MK II VANDEN PLAS

When the revised Mk II version of the ADO16 body shell was introduced in October 1967, the Vanden Plas models of course also took it on. Over the summer of 1967 a number of the 'Mk I' cars had been built with the new 1275cc engine in 58bhp single-carburettor form, and now this became available with twin carburettors and 65bhp in the Vanden Plas 1300. Like the other twin-carburettor A-series engines, it also had double valve springs. The Mk II revisions were also applied to a continuation of the 1100-engined car known as the Vanden Plas 1100 Mk II, but this had a relatively short production life and was discontinued in autumn 1968 after just 1,753 examples had been built. That figure now makes it one of the rarest of all ADO16 derivatives.

There were many more differences between the Mk II and the Mk I than might be imagined, and it was clear that BMC's cost accountants had given the car a thorough going-over. From the

Not much had changed on the outside by the time of the later Vanden Plas models. Dark colours and the upright grille always helped to give this smallest Vanden Plas model an air of gravitas, which was responsible for much of its appeal. Only the side repeater indicator indicates that this is a Mk II model.

outside, only new wheel trims on perforated black disc wheels were in evidence along with the shortened rear wing extensions, although the absence from the brochures of the earlier two-tone colour schemes was telling. Inside, however, the cost-cutting was very obvious. The seats were now upholstered in a combination of leather and Ambla PVC, with a simpler all-over pleating pattern and a shared armrest between the two at the front. The door trims were now of Ambla, too. On the dash, the instruments were less deeply recessed, and there was a new horizontal glovebox handle – introduced, apparently, to meet safety concerns about the earlier type. Though still made of West of England cloth, the headlining was now bonded to a moulded glass fibre pad. Pockets in the seat backs were a bonus,

though, and the walnut picnic tables were still present, along with the polished walnut dash and door cappings.

On its introduction at the October 1967 Earls Court Motor Show, the new Vanden Plas 1300 was priced at £812 with Purchase Tax of £187 16s 1d, making the total £999 16s 1d. It was notable, however, that there was no separate Vanden Plas stand at the Earls Court show in 1968 or 1969. Although sales remained comfortable over the next couple of years, the Mk II models never attained the popularity of the original Mk I cars.

MK III VANDEN PLAS

Once again following the lead of the larger-volume ADO16 derivatives, the Vanden Plas

Not every Vanden Plas model was finished in sombre colours: this Mk III 1300 had a brighter approach to life. Note that the side repeaters have now gone, and that the stainless steel fillet at the trailing edge of the rear quarter-light has also disappeared.

became a Mk III model in September 1971. All the Mk III cars of course had the 1300 engine, and they were very much the same as the Mk II cars they replaced. There were small differences, however.

The only recognition point from the outside – paint colours were unchanged – was that the front wings no longer carried side repeater flashers. Inside, the cars shared the latest heater control panel and bright plastic gear knob with the other Mk III ADO16s, together with the larger foot pedals. A final change came during 1974 when anti-burst door locks were fitted to meet new legislation. The Vanden Plas 1300 finally bowed out in June that year, giving way to the new Vanden Plas 1500, which was based on the Austin Allegro. The very last Vanden Plas Princess 1300 left the assembly lines on 19 June.

Prices had climbed yet again. At launch, a Vanden Plas 1300 Mk III remained far and away the most expensive ADO16 derivative, at £1231.88. This was made up of a £984 base price that was inflated by £247.88 Purchase Tax. Sales nevertheless remained remarkably buoyant, and showed an improvement over their Mk II levels. In 1972 and 1973 the Vanden Plas 1300 actually outsold the cheaper Wolseley version of the ADO16, too.

Dashboards changed very little during the life of the Vanden Plas models. This one is on a 1972 car, and shows the figured wood finish and generally sober approach so typical of the marque.

Leather upholstery, with wood door trim and picnic tables – all were expected in top-quality luxury cars and seemed quite at home in a Vanden Plas ADO16, too. This is again a 1972 model.

Even the badging was discreet on these cars.

ABOVE: **Light colours, such as this white on a 1973 1300 model, made the cars look too much like lesser ADO16s to be in keeping with the Vanden Plas ethos.**

RIGHT: **Discretion again: there is no catchy advertising slogan on the cover of this 1972 sales brochure, just the name of the model and a straightforward picture.**

The Vanden Plas ADO16 went out of production as British Leyland was going into a deep decline and morale within the workforce was sinking fast. Nevertheless, those who had worked on the model ensured that there was some ceremony associated with the last car off the line on 19 June 1974.

PAINT AND TRIM COLOURS

Vanden Plas Princess 1100 Mk I

Body	Interior
Black	Blue Grey or Champagne Beige
Blue Royale	Blue Grey
Carlton Grey	Blue
Chalk Blue	Blue Grey
Connaught Green	Adam Beige or Champagne Beige
Deep Green	Champagne Beige
Midnight Blue	Blue
Peat	Champagne Beige
Sherwood Green	Champagne Beige
Snowberry White	Blue Grey or Cherokee Red
Stone	Blue
Tartan Red	Champagne Beige
Titan Beige	Champagne Beige
Trafalgar Blue	Blue Grey
Yukon Grey	Maroon
Carlton Grey over Midnight Blue	Blue
Sherwood Green over Deep Green	Champagne Beige
Stone over Carlton Grey	Blue

Vanden Plas Princess 1300 Mk II and Mk III

Body	Interior
Antelope	Autumn Leaf
Black	Blue Grey or Champagne Beige
Black Tulip	Navy
Blue Royale	Princess Blue Grey
Carlton Grey	Blue Grey
Connaught Green	Champagne Beige
Damask Red	Black or Navy
Fawn Brown	Champagne Beige
Glacier White	Olive, Navy, Princess Blue Grey or Autumn Leaf
Green Mallard	Limeflower
Harvest Gold	Olive
Limeflower	Limeflower
Midnight Blue	Navy
Mirage	Navy
Peat	Champagne Beige
Racing Green	Champagne Beige
Sherwood Green	Champagne Beige
Snowberry White	Blue Grey
Teal Blue	Olive
Trafalgar Blue	Blue Grey
Wild Moss	Olive or Champagne Beige

VANDEN PLAS PRINCESS 1100 AND 1300 IDENTIFICATION NUMBERS

Car numbers ('chassis' or VIN numbers)
V AS I (from 101)   Princess 1100 Mk I and Mk II
V AS 2 (from 16160)   Princess 1300 Mk II and Mk III
VG ASI   MG Princess

Commission numbers
V 16 S (from 101)   Princess 1100 Mk I
V 16 S (from 16160)   Princess Mk II and Mk III, all
                         types
VG 16 S (from 101)   MG Princess

Body shell codes
VS (from 101)   Princess 1100 Mk I (also MG
                         Princess)
VS (from 1400)   Princess 1300 Mk II and Mk III

Engine codes
10 V   1100 Mk I
12 G, 12 H   1275 Mk I
10H   1100 Mk II
12H   1300 Mk II and Mk III

Typical code:
10V -TAH- 654321
10V is the engine type code
TA indicates standard-ratio gearbox
H indicates High compression (L for Low compression)
654321 is the serial number

On Mk II and Mk III models the engine prefix code is followed by a four-digit code consisting of three numbers and a letter. An example would be 491F, which indicates a twin-carburettor engine with carburettor crankcase ventilation, a Lucas C40 dynamo with negative earth and an all-synchromesh manual gearbox. The H or L code then prefixes the serial number, so that a typical number might be 10V491F-H12345.

VANDEN PLAS PRINCESS 1100 AND 1300 PRODUCTION

These production figures are for calendar-years, and were provided by the manufacturer during its time as the Austin Rover Group.

It is not possible to give individual figures for Mk I versus Mk II production in 1967.

The 1275 models built between April and October 1967 are probably included in the figures for 1100s for that model-year.

The 154 MG Princess models for the USA and elsewhere are probably included in the 1964–6 totals here.

Year	Home	Export	Total	
1964	2,016	440	2,456	
1965	6,316	927	7,243	
1966	3,955	600	4,555	
1967	1,388	318	1,706	(1100)
	998	78	1,076	(1300)
1968	26	21	47	(1100)
	3,226	482	3,708	(1300)
1969	3,064	221	3,285	
1970	3,204	36	3,240	
1971	3,695	0	3,695	
1972	4,518	1	4,519	
1973	3,222	7	3,229	
1974	982	0	982	
	Grand Total		39,741	

WOLSELEY 1100 MK 1

What Wolseley had once been and what it had become under BMC was a sore point with traditional devotees of the marque. Yet by the start of the 1960s the wider public perceived a Wolseley as a well-appointed and relatively discreet car, a cut above the everyday Austins and Morrises but not particularly associated with high performance – even though the bigger Wolseleys had been popular as police cars in the 1940s and 1950s. So that was the brief to which the Wolseley derivative of ADO16 was prepared.

Even though the performance aspect was not important, differentiation among the BMC marques was, and so the Wolseley 1100 was prepared with the 55bhp twin-carburettor engine that was already used in the MG models and would also go into its contemporary, the Riley 1100. That helped to distinguish the Wolseley from its Austin and Morris stablemates. Its use of cross-ply tyres instead of the performance-oriented radials on the MG and new Riley models also spoke volumes for the way BMC perceived the intended audience. It went without saying that only a four-door body style would be offered but, surprisingly, no automatic-transmission version was planned – and least, not yet.

On the outside, the front end was redesigned to incorporate a traditional Wolseley grille, complete with the grille badge that lit up when the sidelights were on – a Wolseley feature since 1933. A pair of horizontal chrome grilles flanked it, each one incorporating a rectangular light unit that contained both turn signal and sidelight and was unique to the Wolseley. Hubcaps with the stylized W for Wolseley pressed into their centres helped further with the marque identity. A vertical number-plate light on either side of the rear number-plate was another Wolseley-only feature, and of course the boot lid carried marque and model name badges.

As two-tone bodywork was popular on models such as the Farina-styled 16/60 and the 1500 that the new Wolseley 1100 would replace, that too became part of the specification. However, the colour split was quite different from the Vanden Plas style, where the roof and roof pillars contrasted with the main body colour. On the Wolseley the main colour covered the lower body sides and the roof, while the contrast colour covered the bonnet, the front panel and the body sides between the windows and the side moulding. This was emphasized by a chrome strip running front to back, with an angled finisher ahead of

The two-tone schemes adopted for the Wolseley models were very attractive, but did date quite quickly. This is an early publicity picture: was the setting chosen to reflect that number-plate?

ABOVE: **A long-established feature of Wolseley cars was a marque badge on the grille that lit up with the sidelights. It was present to the end of the Wolseley ADO16s.**

RIGHT: **It was interesting that Wolseley publicity usually featured young people, as here, when the car was clearly aimed at an older buyer. This sales brochure, covering the full Wolseley range of the time, dates from 1966.**

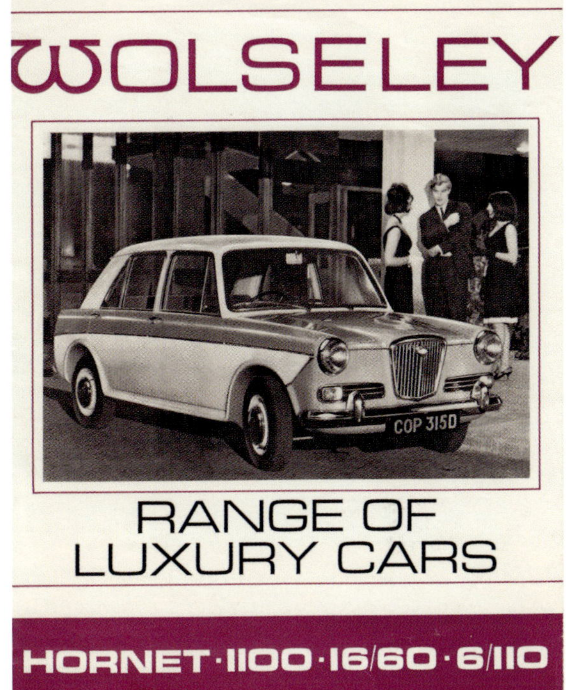

the front wheel arch. With much brighter colours than were generally used on the Vanden Plas, the Wolseley also looked more modern.

Leather upholstery and wood trim were features expected on a Wolseley, too. However, this was not to be the top-quality wood-and-leather of the Vanden Plas 1100: the leather was applied only on the seat facings, and the walnut — lighter-coloured than in the Vanden Plas — was used only for the dashboard and not for the door cappings as well. The dashboard incorporated a strip speedometer like that on the MG 1100, a black-lidded ashtray, and its switchgear was outboard of the speedometer but in the wood itself rather than in a separate switch panel as on the Vanden Plas. The front doors carried useful stowage bins, and the door cards were neatly pleated but very obviously not trimmed in leather.

The Wolseley 1100 was announced at the Earls Court Motor Show in October 1965. There were three examples on the Wolseley stand, one in Trafalgar Blue and Farina Grey and the second in Toga White and Damask Red. The third car was a special show model with no doors or door pillar on its left-hand side; it was displayed on a turntable and was presented in a non-production combination of metallic green with grey seats and scarlet carpets. All had been built at Longbridge, as indeed all the early Wolseley 1100s would be. With two-tone paint, the new car cost £775 9s 2d, made up of a £635 10s 0d base price and Purchase Tax of £139 19s 2d. Single-tone models were, of course, slightly cheaper, while an automatic gearbox added to the cost.

Sales got off to a very strong start, but production figures suggest that they levelled off very rapidly and then began to decline during 1967. Clearly, the novelty of a Wolseley ADO16 had soon begun to wear thin. That may have been one reason why the Wolseley became one of the models on which the 58bhp single-carburettor 1275 engine was tried out over the summer of 1967.

'It is a pity that this replacement for the Wolseley 1500 should cost almost £100 more', commented *Autocar* when it tested a Wolseley 1100 for its 15

Although this looks like an ordinary Mk II Wolseley, the caption on the original press photograph makes clear that it has the 58bhp single-carburettor 1275cc engine that was used only briefly over the summer of 1967.

October 1965 issue. 'Yet it gives considerably better performance and more passenger space, and by its advanced nature the engineering must be more expensive.'

The car had all the familiar 1100 characteristics, but in this case suspension quirks and noise levels were singled out. The limitations of the Hydrolastic system 'are noticed most in traffic, when the front rears up and plunges down more than other cars; and with a tail load of luggage or passengers the bows lift like a speedboat's and send the headlamp beams up into the trees. In these conditions the rear seat ride becomes harsh.' Tyre roar was intrusive, and the car would have benefited from more sound-deadening. In addition, 'the test car's gearbox was the noisiest of any 1100 we have driven, with pronounced gear whine in first and second that resonated right through the car at certain critical speeds, and idler gears that rattled loudly at tick-over'.

Performance was also rather disappointing. The Wolseley managed 20.6 seconds for the 0–60mph standing start and, 'comparing the acceleration with that of the Austin we tested on 18 October 1963, the Wolseley seems to fall about halfway between that and the MG'. At higher speeds, it was not so good: 'acceleration above 70 is sluggish … [and] … calls for intelligent use of the gearbox to make the best of the engine'.

DUTCH WOLSELEY WESP

Back in 1935–6 the Wolseley Wasp had been a bigger-engined derivative of the Wolseley Nine six-light saloon. Thirty years later, the name was revived – in its Dutch form of Wesp – on Wolseley 1100s imported into that country.

The name was the idea of Dirk van der Mark, who ran the Dutch import business for Riley and Wolseley. As the Riley version of the ADO16, released at the same time as the Wolseley, took its Kestrel name from the marque's 1930s heritage, van der Mark thought the Wolseley deserved a name of similar vintage. So the Mk I cars carried Wesp badges and were advertised under that name. Curiously, however, sales brochures never seem to have used it.

MK II WOLSELEYS

The proper Mk II versions of the Wolseley became available in October 1967 after their announcement at the Earls Court show that month. There were both 1100s and new 1300s, although the smaller-engined cars would remain available only until the early spring of 1968. Automatic transmission now became an option on both 1100 and 1300 versions, and during 1968 the 1300 took on the new all-synchromesh manual gearbox, although it retained the original wide ratio spacing. The Wolseleys still retained cross-ply tyres: radials were strictly for the sporting marques. The 1300s had 65bhp and twin carburettors unless fitted with the automatic, when they came with a single-carburettor 60bhp version of the engine. Prices had gone up, of course: a Wolseley 1300 cost £670 plus £155 5s 3d Purchase Tax, or £825 5s 3d in all.

There were three distinguishing features on the outside in addition to the smaller rear wing projections that were part of the Mk II facelift. First, the car now came with side repeater flashers on their front wings; second, there was a new fluted boot lid handle that now incorporated the number-plate lights; and third, the bigger-engined cars carried a 1300 badge on the tail. On the inside, the cost accountants had certainly been at work, but the results were not all bad. If the narrower pleating and other elements of the seat

ABOVE AND LEFT: **Somehow, the Wolseley marque escaped the axe that removed Riley from the BMC stable in 1969. This car is a Mk II 1300 from the 1970 model-year, wearing optional wheel embellisher rings and carrying the side repeater indicator characteristic of the Mk IIs.**

ABOVE: **Badges were discreet, as befitted the Wolseley marque. The bright strip across the boot lid was a distinguishing feature and had been necessary as a border for the paintwork of the two-tone cars.**

RIGHT: **The hubcaps with their embossed W remained unchanged on Mk II models.**

Wolseley owners got the strip speedometer in a wood-veneer dashboard and, of course, leather upholstery. The Wolseley symbol was on both the steering-wheel boss and the gearshift grip. This is a Mk II car.

redesign did have a cheapening effect, the new ruched front door pockets and folding centre rear armrest gave a more expensive feel to the passenger cabin. Most important as far as Wolseley customers were concerned was that the contact surfaces of the seats were still upholstered in leather.

Sales immediately picked up and, though they never quite attained the heights of the Wolseley's early days, they never again dipped as low as they had in 1967. Even exports improved, though more slowly, and in 1969–70 they comfortably exceeded all previous export figures for the Wolseley derivatives of ADO16.

The ruched door pockets – again on a Mk II – were a neat touch, and the door trims did look a little more upmarket than those in Austin and Morris versions of the time.

The twin-carburettor 1300 A-series engine carried a Wolseley identification sticker, although it was just that – on this engine it has started to peel off.

MK III WOLSELEYS

In September 1971 the Wolseley 1300 became a Mk III model, sharing most of the innovations introduced for the other ADO16s: the new plastic gear knob, plastic heater panel, deeper pile carpets, smaller sun visors and larger pedals. The rectangular British Leyland badge was attached below the trim strip on the left-hand wing only, as on other Mk IIIs.

Other specification changes reflected BL's attempts to save manufacturing costs: the indicator repeater lights had disappeared from the front wings, the passenger cabin had lost the acoustic padding from its D-pillars, while the boot now had a painted hardboard floor instead of one trimmed in vinyl. Showroom costs were rising, and the Mk III Wolseley was announced with a total price of £993.13, which consisted of a £793 base price and

PAINT AND TRIM COLOURS

In the Duotone combinations, the first colour shown was for the roof and lower body; the second colour was for the contrast panels at waist height. As elsewhere, BMC were not always consistent in their listing of Maroon, which sometimes appeared under its name of Maroon B. The two colours were the same.

This table was compiled with considerable assistance from Anders Clausager.

Mk I, 1965–7

Body	Interior
Farina Grey	Reef Blue
Glen Green	Green
Maroon	Heron Grey
Trafalgar Blue	Reef Blue
Farina Grey over Maroon	Heron Grey
Farina Grey over Trafalgar Blue	Reef Blue
Glen Green over Spruce Green	Green
Trafalgar Blue over Black	Reef Blue

By February 1967, the range had been expanded by one option:

Body	Interior
Black	Green

Mk II 1300, 1967–8

The final Mk I colour range was carried over for the early Mk II cars. From approximately May 1968, Farina Grey was dropped, and with it the two Duotone options in which it featured. This left a colour range of four single-tone and two Duotone options.

Mk II 1300, September 1968 to late 1970

Body	Interior
Bermuda Blue	Black
Connaught Green	Black
Cumulus Grey	Galleon Blue
Damask Red	Icon Red
Faun Brown	Mushroom
Sandy Beige	Mushroom
Snowberry White	Black
Trafalgar Blue	Galleon Blue

Note: Although the colour was now described as Faun Brown, it was in fact the same as the earlier Fawn Brown. All the Duotone options had now been discontinued.

Mk II 1300, late 1970 to July 1971

Body	Interior
Bedouin	Autumn Leaf
Damask Red	Navy
Flame Red	Navy
Glacier White	Navy or Geranium
Limeflower	Navy or Limeflower
Midnight Blue	Navy or Geranium
Racing Green	Limeflower
Wild Moss	Olive

Mk III 1300, August to October 1971

Body	Interior
Aqua	Navy
Black Tulip	Geranium
Blaze	Navy
Bronze Yellow	Navy
Green Mallard	Limeflower
Harvest Gold	Olive
Teal Blue	Limeflower

Note: The August 1971 colour chart listed the same colours as those from late 1970, plus a new selection as shown above. In addition, Glacier White from the 'old' paint chart was now listed with the addition of Autumn Leaf as a third interior colour. The Mk IIIs were not announced until

September 1971, and it may be that they were available only in the new colours and that the old colours were listed to cover the continuing availability of old-stock Mk II cars.

Mk III 1300, November 1971 to August 1972

Body	Interior
Aqua	Navy
Black Tulip	Geranium
Blaze	Navy
Bronze Yellow	Navy
Flame Red	Navy
Glacier White	Autumn Leaf or Navy
Green Mallard	Limeflower
Harvest Gold	Olive
Limeflower	Limeflower
Midnight Blue	Navy or Geranium
Teal Blue	Limeflower

Mk III 1300, from September 1972

Body	Interior
Aqua	Navy
Black Tulip	Navy or Geranium
Blaze	Navy
Bronze Yellow	Navy
Damask Red (new)	Navy
Flame Red	Navy
Glacier White	Olive or Autumn Leaf or Navy
Green Mallard	Limeflower
Harvest Gold	Olive
Limeflower	Limeflower
Midnight Blue	Navy or Geranium
Teal Blue	Olive or Limeflower

Note: By February 1973, the Wolseley 1300 was no longer listed in British Leyland paint charts.

This was the final iteration of the Wolseley, a Mk III model from late 1971. The side repeater indicators have gone, and there is now a British Leyland emblem on the front wing, just ahead of the door.

£200.13 in Purchase Tax. This price was, incidentally, exactly the same as that of the sporting MG 1300.

Home market sales bore up well for the first year of Mk III production, but overall production was greatly reduced because the Wolseley was no longer offered in export markets. (In fact, four were made for export in 1972–3, perhaps to special order.) Bright new colours reflected the mood of the 1970s, but the Wolseley 1300 was not destined to last long. Production was halted in April 1973 and the model was not directly replaced within the British Leyland range. The Wolseley name itself lapsed in 1975, last appearing on short-lived but well-equipped 6-cylinder versions of the latest 18/22 wedge-shaped saloons.

Although Riley models had been withdrawn earlier in the year, the Wolseley that had been introduced at the same time remained in production in August 1969. British Leyland clearly felt they needed to remind buyers of the fact. The small print admits that those driving lamps cost extra.

WOLSELEY 1100 AND 1300 IDENTIFICATION NUMBERS

Car numbers ('chassis' or VIN numbers)

W AS 1	1100 Mk I and Mk II
W AS 4	1275 and 1300 Mk II
W AS 4S5	1300 Mk II and Mk III

These prefix codes are followed by a serial number, and the serial number is followed by an A (Longbridge assembly) or an M (Cowley assembly). A full number might therefore read W AS 4 56789 M.

Commission numbers

W 16 S (from 101)	Mk I
W 16 S (from 15189)	1300
W 16 S (from 20562)	1300 Mk II and Mk III

The serial number is followed by an L (Longbridge assembly) or an M (Cowley assembly). A full number might therefore read W 16S 501 L.

Body shell codes

WS 101	Mk I
WS 13600	Mk II and Mk III

The serial number is followed by an L or a P. A full number might therefore read WS 501 L.

Engine codes

10GRB	1100 Mk I
12G, 12H	1275 Mk I
10H	1100 Mk II
12H	1300 Mk II and Mk III

On Mk I models the engine prefix code is followed by a transmission type code and an H (High compression) or an L (Low compression). The final segment of an engine number is then the serial number, so that a full number might read 10GRB-TAH54321. The most common transmission type codes were TA (standard-ratio manual gearbox) and A (automatic gearbox).

On Mk II and Mk III models, the engine prefix code is followed by a four-digit code consisting of three numbers and a letter. Typical would be 209C, which indicates twin carburettors, a 22-amp dynamo, crankcase ventilation and standard-ratio gearbox. The H or L code then prefixes the serial number, so that a typical number might be 10H209C-H67890.

WOLSELEY 1100 AND 1300 PRODUCTION

These production figures are for calendar-years, and were provided by the manufacturer during its time as the Austin Rover Group.

Year	Home	Export	Total	
1965	7,240	346	7,526	
1966	5,524	1,158	6,682	
1967	2,601	247	2,848	(1100)
	533	29	562	(1300)
1968	37	211	248	(1100)
	5,020	430	5,450	(1300)
1969	4,174	1,619	5,793	
1970	3,282	1,643	4,925	
1971	3,945	1,158	5,103	
1972	4,515	3	4,518	
1973	1,064	1	1,065	
		Grand Total	44,720	

Technical Specifications, Vanden Plas and Wolseley ADO16 saloons

Engine
1100 models
BMC A-series 4-cylinder, with iron block and cylinder
head
1098cc (64.58 × 83.72mm)
Overhead valves; chain-driven camshaft
Three-bearing crankshaft
Compression ratio 8.5:1
Two SU HS2 carburettors with manual gearbox; HS4
with automatic
55bhp at 5,500rpm
61 lb ft at 2,500rpm

1275 models
BMC A-series 4-cylinder, with iron block and cylinder
head
1275cc (70.6 × 81.28mm)
Overhead valves; chain-driven camshaft
Three-bearing crankshaft
Compression ratio 8.8:1
One SU HS4 carburettor
58bhp at 5,250rpm
69 lb ft at 3,000rpm

1300 models
BMC A-series 4-cylinder, with iron block and cylinder
head
1275cc (70.6 × 81.28mm)
Overhead valves; chain-driven camshaft
Three-bearing crankshaft
Compression ratio 9.75:1
Two SU HS2 carburettors with manual gearbox; HS4
with automatic
65bhp at 5,750rpm
71 lb ft at 3,000rpm

Transmission
Four-speed manual gearbox, with no synchromesh on
first gear with synchromesh on all forward gears from
mid-1968
Gear ratios   (1100): 3.63:1, 2.17:1, 1.41:1, 1.00:1,
                reverse 3.63:1
                (1275 and 1300): 3.52:1, 2.22:1, 1.43:1,
                1.00:1, reverse 3.54:1
Four-speed AP automatic gearbox optional on 1100 Mk
II and 1300 models of both marques; gear ratios 2.69:1,
1.85:1, 1.46:1, 1,00:1, reverse 2.69
Front-wheel drive

Axle ratio
1100: 4.13:1
1275: 3.44:1 (early models); 3.65:1 (late models)

1300: 3.65:1
1300 automatic: 3.76:1

Suspension, steering and brakes
All-round independent suspension with Hydrolastic
units, interconnected front to rear. Front suspension
with wishbones; rear suspension with trailing arms and
anti-roll bar
Rack-and-pinion steering
Front disc brakes and rear drum brakes. Servo
assistance on Vanden Plas 1300

Dimensions
Overall length	12ft 2.7in (3,726mm)
Overall width	5ft 0.4in (1534mm)
Overall height	4ft 4.7in (1,338mm)
Wheelbase	7ft 9.5in (2,375mm)
Front track	4ft 3.5in (1,308mm)
Rear track	4ft 2.9in (1,292mm)

Wheels and tyres
12-inch steel disc wheels, with 4-inch rims
5.50x12 cross-ply tyres
145x12 radial tyres (available from 1968)

Unladen weights
Wolseley 1100	1,820lb (825kg) approx
Vanden Plas 1100	1,950lb (884kg) approx
Vanden Plas 1300	2,015lb (914kg) approx

Performance and fuel
Vanden Plas 1100
0–60mph	21.1 sec
Maximum	85mph (136.8km/h)
Fuel consumption	31mpg (9.13ltr/100km)

Wolseley 1100
0–60mph	18.4 sec
Maximum	85mph (136.8km/h)
Fuel consumption	29mpg (9.76ltr/100km)

Wolseley 1275
0–60mph	17.3 sec
Maximum	88mph (141.6km/h)
Fuel consumption	30mpg (9.43ltr/100km)

Wolseley 1300 MkII
0–60mph	14.1 sec
Maximum	93mph (149.7km/h)
Fuel consumption	27mpg (10.48ltr/100km)

CHAPTER SEVEN

BUILT ABROAD:
THE OVERSEAS MODELS

Even though the vast majority of ADO16s were built at the BMC factories in the UK, a significant number of cars were built abroad. Many were actually shipped overseas as kits of parts for local assembly. Such kits were known as KD types (the letters stand for Knocked Down) and were produced for a variety of reasons.

KD operations were nothing new, and in fact Ford had been running such operations as long ago as the early 1920s. By the 1960s they were quite common in both developed and undeveloped countries. Like other car manufacturers, BMC used them as a way of getting their products into countries where they would otherwise be unsaleable.

Typically, a foreign government might protect its domestic economy by placing high import taxes on vehicles brought in from overseas; this would effectively price the vehicles out of the market and so discourage imports. On the other hand, a government might encourage in-territory assembly of vehicles because this provided work for the local labour force. Over a period of time, it might also teach them the skills needed to progress towards an indigenous motor industry. In many cases, items such as tyres, glass, paint and batteries were sourced locally, and this too contributed to the local economy.

ADO16s were assembled from KD kits in a number of overseas territories. These included Australia, Belgium, Ireland, New Zealand, the Philippines, Rhodesia, Portugal, South Africa and Spain. The Australian and South African operations progressed to developing ADO16 derivatives of their own, and, along with the Spanish operation, eventually undertook virtually complete local

manufacture. There were unique arrangements for ADO16 manufacture in Chile. Meanwhile, in Italy, BMC had a relationship with local manufacturer Innocenti, who built its own derivatives of the ADO16 under licence.

AUSTRALIA

Australian buyers were attuned to the Morris marque, because the Nuffield Organisation had established a large presence there in the years immediately after the Second World War. Right from the start, Nuffield's plan was to work towards full local manufacture. The first stage in achieving that was to have bodies built in Australia while all the other parts were supplied from the UK. By the mid-1950s engines and gearboxes were also being manufactured locally, and within a few years the Australian arm of BMC was developing and building its own derivatives of the UK designs to suit the local market.

The Australians were rightly proud of the engineering capability they had developed, and BMC was not about to challenge their knowledge of what their own domestic market wanted. Beginning in late 1963, some UK-built 1100s were shipped out to Australia to act as prototypes for the Australian-specification cars. They were hand-modified and tested over a period of around eighteen months before the actual launch on 17 February 1964.

The Australian-built 1100s were far more unlike their UK counterparts than they appeared at first sight. The most obvious difference was that these cars had a bench front seat. To make way for this, there was a long cranked gear lever, while the hand-

Australians were attuned to the US system of giving engines attractive-sounding names, and the earliest 1100s built in that country carried the name of FireFlash, which is just visible on this example where the marque name would normally be.

brake was relocated between the driver's side of the seat and the door. The doors lost their oddments bins and gained armrests, which on the front doors were adjustable. An Australian-made air-blending heater, without a booster fan, was added and the control switches on the facia were given identifying letters. Interior trim changed to dimpled PVC and leathercloth, rubber flooring replaced the carpets and the boot also gained a special rubber mat.

Not surprisingly, special attention was paid to dust-sealing, and the Australian-built cars differed from their UK counterparts in this respect. There were stone shields under the car to protect the fuel pump and fuel tank, and the final drive was changed to a lower 4.26:1 in order to give the car better top-gear acceleration. The gearbox ratios were unchanged, though, and the car was still capable of a 77mph top speed. Under the bonnet, the engine carried the brand name FireFlash where UK types had the marque name. On the outside, the boot release and number-plate lights were different from the UK types, and front and rear over-riders were standard. An external visor could be bought as an option to protect front seat occupants from glare, and a metal-slatted Venetian blind was available to fit inside the rear window and protect the rear passengers from the sun.

This satisfied the Australian market for the next five years, but in the meantime the Australian engineers had been looking at making the car more suitable for local conditions. During 1966 they worked with their counterparts at Longbridge to develop a five-door hatchback body derivative. There was no call for this on the UK market, which was to receive the similarly specified but larger Austin Maxi in 1969, but the model did enter production in Australia with the internal development code of YDO9.

First, however, there would be a further development of the Morris 1100 for Australia. This was a 1275cc-engined version with the four-speed AP automatic as standard, and it was badged as a Morris 1100S. This name was probably chosen to avoid confusion, for this was an up-engined 1100 and what was coming next needed to be quite clearly distinguished from it. The 1100S was built between August 1967 and June 1969, at which date all Australian ADO16 production ceased. Nearly 90,000 examples had been built.

The Australian factories immediately began production of a replacement range, which consisted of two models derived from ADO16. The four-door saloon, which featured a body shell with cut-back rear wings like those on the Mk II ADO16 models, was known internally as the YDO15. The five-door hatchback, YDO9, was marketed as the Morris Nomad.

Each model could be had with two different engines. The four-door saloon came as a Morris

The hatchback derivative of the ADO16 was practical, although in side view it did look a little odd. The Australians liked it, though, taking it on under the designation of **YDO9** and selling it as a Morris Nomad. The letter-box door handles are clear in this picture.

Five-door practicality, Australian-style. In fact, the basic body design for YDO9 was made in the UK. If those rear lights look familiar, there is a reason: they were borrowed from the Wolseley 18/85 Mk I.

1300 Auto, with a specification broadly similar to that of the discontinued 1100S, or as a re-engined Morris 1500 OHC – a model unique to Australia. The YDO15s had flap-type door handles in bright metal and a front end with a big grille and large indicator-and-sidelight units that made them look very different from the UK-built ADO16s of the time. Both had expanded vinyl upholstery with a bench front seat as standard, which meant that the handbrake lever had to be relocated between the driver's seat and the door. Both had Smiths ribbon-type speedometers, and both came with reinforced sub-frames and a sump guard as standard to protect against damage from unmade Australian roads. A stone-guard for the rear sub-frame was an extra-cost option. Both four-door YDO15s also

ENGINEERING TECHNICAL DATA

GENERAL DATA

D.O. Ref	YDO.9 - 1300 Auto
Model	Morris Nomad 1300 Automatic
Body Type	5 Door Saloon. (12H.169/H-(EX-UK)
Engine	4 Cylinder O.H.V. Type(12YE/A/H-(LOCAL).
Bore	2.78 ins. (70.61 m.m.)
Stroke	3.20 ins. (81.28 m.m.)
Cubic Capacity	1275 c.c. (77.9. cu.in.)
Compression Ratio	8.6 :1
Brake Horse Power	63 B.H.P. @ 5500 R.P.M.
RAC H.P. rating	12.4
Torque	70 lb.ft. @ 2500 R.P.M.
Firing Order	1, 3, 4, 2.
Valve rocker clearance	.012 ins. Hot (.305m.m.)
Spark Plugs	Champion N9Y - 14 m.m.
Spark Plug Gap	.025 ins. (.635m.m.)
Ignition Timing	5° B.T.D.C. @ 500 R.P.M.
Idle Speed	650 R.P.M. Max.
Contact Breaker Gap	.014 - .016 ins.
Carburetter	Single SU - HS 4
Carburetter Needle	DZ-Std.
Carburetter Spring	Red
Fuel Pump	Mechanical
Convertor Max. Torque multiplication figure	2.0 :1

Transmission Ratio	Convertor Output	Gear train	Final Drive	Overall Ratio
First	1.15	2.69	3.273 (22/72)	10.12
Second	1.15	1.85	3.273	6.93
Third	1.15	1.46	3.273	5.48
Fourth	1.15	1.00	3.273	3.76
Reverse	1.15	2.69	3.273	10.12

M.P.H. 1000 r.p.m. Top Gear	16.35
Wheel Size	4 3/8 x 12 Dev.
Tyre Size (Tubeless)	6.20 x 12 x 4 Ply Low Profile.
Tyre Pressure: Normal Conditions: Front	26 lb/sq.in.
Rear	26 lb/sq.in.
Full Load: Front	-
Rear	-
Capacities: Fuel Tank	10 Gallons.
Engine and Transmission oil capacity (including filter)	13 Pints Dry - 9 Pints Wet.
Cooling System (less heater)	7 Pints inc. Exp. Tank
Dimensions: Track (Front)	51.50 ins. (on ground @ Trim Height 13,
Track (Rear)	51.00 ins. 5/8ins
Turning Circle (Between Kerbs)	37 ft. - (Between Walls - 38ft. 5 ins.)
Front Wheel Alignment (Static Unladen)	1/16ins. Toe Out (@ Trim Hight 13.5/8i
Rear Wheel Alignment (" ")	1/8ins. Toe Out (" " ")
Wheel base	93.50 ins.
Overall - Height	54.56 ins.
Overall - Width	60.31 ins.
Overall - Length	147.66 ins.
Ground Clearance	6½ ins.
Approach Angle	21½°
Departure Angle	22½°
Weights: Kerbside Weight (full fuel tank)	2070 lbs.
Registration Weight (2 gal. fuel)	2008 lbs.
G.V.W.	2850 lb.
Tare	-
Maximum Towing Weight.	-

DETAILS OF MODIFICATIONS	AUTHORITY	DETAILS OF MODIFICATIONS	AUTHORITY
RELEASE REVISED: WEIGHTS AND PETROL TAN. CAPACITY ADDED	ECS.26851 ECS.27544	REVISED: ENGINE CODING	ECS.27739.

ABOVE AND OPPOSITE: **There was a full engineering team in place at the Australian assembly plant, which adapted ADO16 to suit local conditions from the start. These pages, dating from 1969, show the general engineering specifications of the YDO9 or Morris Nomad in 1300 form, and of the YDO15, the later Morris 1300 Automatic. Note that the 1300 engines were dual-sourced: those with a 12H prefix came from the UK, but those with a 12YE prefix were manufactured in Australia.**

ENGINEERING TECHNICAL DATA
SUMMARY OF
GENERAL DATA

D.O. Ref	YDO.15 - 1300 Auto.
Model	Morris - 1300 Automatic
Body Type	4 Door Saloon. (12H.169/H-(Ex-UK.)
Engine	4 Cyl. O.H.V. Type 12YE/A/H -(LOCAL).
Bore	2.78ins. (70.61m.m.)
Stroke	3.20 ins. (81.28m.m.)
Cubic Capacity	1275c.c. (77.9 cu.in.)
Compression Ratio	8.6 :1
Brake Horse Power	63 B.H.P. @ 5500 RPM.
RAC H.P. rating	12.4
Torque	70 lb.ft. @ 2500 R.P.M.
Firing Order	1, 3, 4, 2.
Valve rocker clearance	.012 ins. Hot (.305 m.m.)
Spark Plugs	Champion N9Y - 14m.m.
Spark Plug Gap	.025 ins. (.635m.m.)
Ignition Timing	5° B.T.D.C. @ 500 R.P.M.
Idle Speed	650 R.P.M. Max.
Contact Breaker Gap	.014 - .016 ins.
Carburetter	Single SU HS4.
Carburetter Needle	DZ-STD.
Carburetter Spring	Red
Fuel Pump	Mechanical
Convertor Max. Torque multiplication figure	2.0 :1

Transmission Ratio	Convertor Output	Gear train	Final Drive	Overall Ratio
First	1.15	2.69	3.273 (22/72)	10.12
Second	1.15	1.85	3.273	6.93
Third	1.15	1.46	3.273	5.48
Fourth	1.15	1.00	3.273	3.76
Reverse	1.15	2.69	3.273	10.12

M.P.H. 1000 r.p.m. Top Gear	16.35
Wheel Size	4 3/8 x 12 Dev.
Tyre Size (Tubeless)	6.20 x 12 x 4 Ply Low Profile
Tyre Pressure: Normal Conditions: Front	26 lb/sq. ins.
Rear	26 lb/sq. ins.
Full Load: Front	-
Rear	-
Capacities: Fuel Tank	8½ Gallons
Engine and Transmission oil capacity (including filter)	13 pints Dry - 9 pints Wet.
Cooling System (less heater)	7 pints inc. Exp. Tank
Dimensions: Track (Front)	51.50ins. (on ground at Trim Height 13 5/8ins
Track (Rear)	51.00ins.
Turning Circle (Between Kerbs)	37ft.-(Between Walls - 38ft. 5 ins.)
Front Wheel Alignment(Static Unladen)	1/16ins. Toe Out (@ Trim Height 13,5/8i
Rear Wheel Alignment(" ")	1/8ins. Toe Out (" " 13,5/8in
Wheel base	93.50 ins.
Overall - Height	53.00 ins.
Overall - Width	60.38 ins.
Overall - Length	145.60 ins.
Ground Clearance	6½ ins.
Approach Angle	21°
Departure Angle	22½°
Weights: Kerbside Weight (full fuel tank)	1941 lbs.
Registration Weight (2 gal. fuel)	1895 lbs.
G.V.W.	-
Tare	-
Maximum Towing Weight.	-

DETAILS OF MODIFICATIONS	AUTHORITY	DETAILS OF MODIFICATIONS	AUTHORITY
RELEASE	ECS.26851	REVISED: ENGINE CODING.	ECS. 27739.
REVISED: WEIGHTS AND PETROL TANK CAPACITY ADDED	ECS.27544		

came with wider cross-ply tyres in a 6.20 × 12 size (UK-built ADO16s had now switched to radials).

The 1300 Auto had the 1275cc engine with a single HS4 carburettor and 8.6:1 compression ratio, giving 63bhp at 5,500rpm and 70 lb ft at 2,500rpm, and a 3.273:1 final drive. The new 1500 OHC, however, was unique to Australia, and its central feature was the new 1485cc overhead camshaft E-series engine that had been designed for the Maxi. This had a four-point mounting rather than the three-point type of the smaller engines, and demanded a new bonnet with a bulge to make room for the taller OHC engine. All the first cars came with the Maxi's four-speed cable-operated gearbox, but for the 1971 model-year an overdrive five-speed alternative was introduced, again borrowed from the Maxi. These later cars were distinguished by a stainless steel bodyside strip, and by O/D5 badges on each front wing. Both four-speed and five-speed types had the same 3.938:1 final drive, and both were quite a lot heavier than a typical UK-built ADO16. The 1500 models had the Morris name in large letters across the leading edge of the bonnet, and their boot lids carried full '1500 OHC' badging.

The range structure for the hatchback Nomad was essentially the same. The cheaper model was a Nomad 1300 Auto, while the more expensive one was a Nomad 1500 with a choice between four-speed and five-speed manual gearboxes. Again, the final drives were 3.273:1 on the 1300 Auto and 3.938:1 on the 1500, regardless of gearbox type. The Nomad stood slightly taller than an ADO16 at 54.56in (1,386mm), much of the difference probably being down to its bigger tyres. It was an inch or so longer than the four-door saloon, at 147.66in (3,750mm), and it was considerably heavier at 2,094lb (950kg) for the 1300 Auto. Like the saloons, Nomads had no over-riders either front or rear; they also had tail lights unique to ADO16 derivatives, exactly the same as those used on the contemporary Wolseley 18/85 model.

Australian Motor Manual was impressed with the four-speed Morris 1500 when it tested one for its July 1969 issue, describing it as 'something more than just a new engine in an old body shell'. This car and the new Nomad, announced at the same time, 'will be sure to improve the already strong hold BMC has on the medium-small segment of the car market'. The 1500 was 'a better car in every respect and answers practically every criticism aimed at the 1100 series it will ultimately replace'.

> To drive, the 1500 feels like a cross between an 1800 and an 1100 ... Road noise in our test car was minimal, but exhaust resonance at certain speeds seemed to be a problem not yet ironed out ... The 1500's slight extra weight forward of the front wheels tends to add to the understeer, but the wider tyres provide better adhesion. Still, a power-on full chat attack on a tight corner requires plenty of lock before the car accepts your chosen line.'

The more powerful engine made the car 'quite flexible and ... content to dribble along at low speeds in top gear, responding willingly to an opening throttle'. Its new sub-frames gave it 'a feeling of overall tautness that the 1100 doesn't have', and larger front disc brakes with swinging calipers gave better stopping, 'but we tend to disagree mildly with BMC's claim that servo assistance is still not necessary'. The magazine recorded 15.4 seconds for the 0–60mph sprint and a top speed of 88mph.

In time for the 1971 model-year, Leyland Australia altered the primary gear ratio from 1:1 to 1:1.067 and this improved acceleration. *Australian Motor Manual* was quite startled to find that the five-speed 1500 OHC it tested in August 1970 was much quicker through the gears than its earlier four-speed, but appeared not to have registered the change of gearing! That five-speed car needed just 12.2 seconds to hit 60mph, and went on to a top speed of 91mph (146.4km/h). The five-speed gearbox was big news in Australia, where 'until now, five-speed motoring has always been confined to the luxury class' and the new Morris 'makes claim to being the first five-speeder offered to the Australian public at an economy price'. Although gear selection was 'stiff and rather notchy' (a common problem with the Maxi gearbox), it was nonetheless positive. The wood-grain gearshift grip had uncomfortably sharp edges, but 'it is now quieter and easier for the 1500 to cruise and we found it could effortlessly sit at 80mph all day'.

Technical Specifications, Morris 1500 (YDO15)

Engine
British Leyland E-series 4-cylinder, with iron block and cylinder head
1485cc (76 × 81mm)
Overhead camshaft; chain-driven camshaft
Five-bearing crankshaft
Compression ratio 8.6:1
One SU HS4 carburettor
73bhp at 5,500rpm
81 lb ft at 4,000rpm

Transmission
Four-speed manual gearbox, with synchromesh on all forward gears: gear ratios 3.20:1, 2.00:1, 1.37:1, 1,00:1, reverse 3.46:1
Alternative five-speed manual gearbox, with synchromesh on all forward gears: gear ratios 3.20:1, 2.00:1, 1.37:1, 1,00:1, 0.79:1, reverse 3.46:1
Front-wheel drive

Axle ratio
3.938:1

Suspension, steering and brakes
All-round independent suspension with Hydrolastic units, interconnected front to rear. Front suspension with wishbones; rear suspension with trailing arms and anti-roll bar
Rack-and-pinion steering
Front disc brakes and rear drum brakes

Dimensions:

Overall length	13ft 2.6in (4,030mm)
Overall width	5ft 0.4in (1,534mm)
Overall height	4ft 4.7in (1,340mm)
Wheelbase	7ft 9.5in (2,375mm)
Front track	4ft 3.5in (1,308mm)
Rear track	4ft 2.9in (1,292mm)

Wheels and tyres
Steel disc wheels
6.20 × 12 cross-ply tyres

Kerb weight

1500 five-speed car	1,952lb (885.4kg)
1500 Nomad	2,094lb (950kg)

A 1500S version was planned and the press were told that it would have a twin-carburettor version of the engine with 78bhp at 5,750rpm and 84 lb ft at 3,500rpm. However, this was cancelled in November 1969, most likely because initial public reaction to the new models had been disappointing, despite the positive press reception. The 1500 and Nomad were failing to achieve the sales levels of their ADO16 predecessors.

So the four models – 1300 Auto and 1500 OHC, plus their Nomad equivalents – lasted in production for just two years. For the second of these years the four-door saloons were available with an extra-cost enhancement known as the Luxury Pack or LP, which included bucket front seats, extra soundproofing, a wood-grain dash with extra padding and more luxurious carpeting. Production came to an end in 1971, the replacement model being a version of the Morris Marina that carried Leyland badges and had a different range of engines from the UK-built cars.

CHILE

The car assembly situation in Chile during the 1960s was both complex and bizarre. BMC had links with EMSSA in Arica, which also assembled Chevrolet models but was closed down in 1966. After refunding was arranged, it started up again in 1969 as a directly controlled British Leyland subsidiary called British Leyland Automotores de Chile SA.

Arica had been chosen as the site of a new industrial complex by the Chilean government, but was not ideally situated for car manufacture because it was more than 1,600 miles from the Chilean iron, steel and glass industry centred on Concepción and

Talcahuano. To overcome the problem, British Leyland decided to manufacture bodies in Chile from GRP, and in 1969 it began production of a GRP-bodied Mini 1000. The aim was to follow this with GRP-bodied versions of the two-door MG 1300. Much of the vehicle's strength was to come from steel tubing. This combination would meet the Chilean government requirement for a minimum of 55 per cent local or at least South American content. Engines and other mechanical components were to be shipped out from the UK, and the cars were to be built in a new factory.

However, there were problems from the start with the Chilean ADO16 operation. British Leyland engineers were sent out to develop the fibreglass body, but discovered that the promised new factory had not been built. They nevertheless managed to get a prototype up and running within three months, and six months later were ready to begin volume production. In practice, however, production did not begin until 1971. When the car was introduced, the official publicity line was that fibreglass bodywork had been chosen because of the local humidity – no doubt a face-saving explanation designed to appease the Allende government of the time.

Production of MG 1300s with fibreglass bodies ran until 1974, when the factory was closed down by the military government of Augusto Pinochet that replaced the left-wing Allende government in September 1973. The Heritage Motor Centre collection in Britain has a 1973 Chilean-built GRP car that wears Morris badges, and may have been intended as a prototype, and there is a colourful account of the early days of the operation on AROnline (www.aronline.co.uk), written by Rodrigo Toledo, one of the engineers involved.

ITALY

The Italian engineering company of Innocenti signed an agreement with BMC during 1959 to assemble the British company's cars for the Italian market from CKD kits at its factory in Milan. Part of the agreement was that Innocenti could develop the cars further to suit its market, and the Austin A40 was modified in a number of ways after production began in 1960. Innocenti put its own name on these cars and on a completely rebodied derivative of the Austin-Healey Sprite that was sold as an Innocenti 950. By the time A40 production ended, Innocenti had progressed from CKD to full local manufacture.

The ADO16 was taken on primarily as a replacement for the A40, and the first version from the Italian maker was a four-door model called the IM3. The name stood for Innocenti-Morris and the 3 indicated that this was the third car from the BMC collaboration. Production began in April 1963 and the cars had a number of differences from the UK-built Morris 1100. Most obvious were headlamp units that incorporated the side and indicator lamps and resembled the shape of those on the A40; this was probably a deliberate ploy to give the two cars a family resemblance. The side trim strip also differed, stopping short of the rear wing, and the fuel filler was concealed under a neat flap. Bumpers also differed from those on UK cars, and chrome flashes on the bonnet and sides were perhaps inspired by similar features on Pininfarina's original styling model for the ADO16.

The IM3 came with the twin-carburettor 1100 engine from the MG 1100, boosted to 58bhp by different carburettor needles, and could be had with either the standard Morris gearbox or a 'sport gearbox' option. It also came with a brake servo and with perforated wheel discs that carried special hubcaps. The electrical system was of Italian design and far more sophisticated than BMC's own, with a bigger fusebox, relays for headlamps and horns, boot and engine bay lights, a low fuel warning light, and even a windscreen wash-wipe system operated by a pedal on the toeboard. There were reversing lights, too, integrated with the number-plate illumination on either side of a unique boot handle and number-plate bracket assembly.

The IM3 had a rather better-appointed passenger cabin than the Morris 1100 on which it was based; the front seats were fully adjustable and on early cars had cloth upholstery, although later ones had vinyl. Twin courtesy lights and heel mats for all four occupants were further features. The dashboard carried two round dials mounted in a very

Italianate layout and generally had fuller instrumentation. The IM3 also had a much more comfortably angled steering wheel than the parent ADO16, thanks to Innocenti's insertion of a pair of universal joints in the steering column. It cost the equivalent of £742 when first announced. Innocenti claimed a top speed of 90mph – 5mph faster than the UK-built MG 1100 of the time.

It was replaced in July 1966 by an improved model called the IM3S, which had the same engine specification and always seems to have had the standard-ratio gearbox. The engines in these cars were sometimes fitted with Italian-made Dell'Orto FZD carburettors instead of the SU HS2 types.

These models had no over-riders, and came with a different grille design.

Meanwhile, a new model call the I4 (fourth Innocenti model) had been introduced at the Turin Motor Show in March 1964. This had the 50bhp single-carburettor 1100 engine and was visually much more similar to the UK-built ADO16. It had the Morris-style grille with eight straight bars flanked by sidelamp-and-indicator units of similar appearance to the UK types, but with clear lenses for the indicators to meet Italian regulations. From mid-1965 it was joined by an I4S model, this time with the 58bhp twin-carburettor engine that again came with either SU or Dell'Orto carburettors.

At first sight the Inncoenti I4 looks like an ordinary ADO16. Look, though, at the different over-riders, sidelights, perforated wheels (this car pre-dates the UK-built Mk IIs), hubcaps and bonnet badge. The door mirror is unlike anything seen in the UK, either, and the trim strip along the door bottoms is uniquely Italian. The side repeater flasher was an Italian-market requirement, and is quite different from the type used on Mk II models built in the UK. LUCI06/WIKIMEDIA COMMONS

This is the Innocenti 15, dating from 1972. Although the grille has been updated, it is not the same as on contemporary Mk III models built in the UK: the Innocenti plate badge sees to that. Wheels are different, too. The flap for the concealed fuel filler that was always an Innocenti feature is also visible here.

All of these models ended production in mid-1970, but not before they had picked up badging changes to become Leyland Innocenti models after British Leyland took over in 1968. In late 1970 or early 1971 Innocenti then began manufacture of their 15 model. This continued to use what Britons knew as the Mk I style of body with its longer rear wings; Innocenti saw no reason to change the tooling they had been using successfully since 1963. The model was readily recognizable by its Rostyle pressed steel wheels. The 15 again came with the 58bhp twin-carburettor 1100 engine, again with either British or Italian-made carburettors. Innocenti embarked on a major export push at about this time, but it is not clear whether the 15 was among those cars it sold outside Italy.

One way or the other, the 15 lasted only until September 1974. Sales had already slowed down. British Leyland had by this time assumed full ownership of the company, buying it for around £3 million during 1972, and Innocenti became a casualty when the parent company ran into a financial crisis at the end of 1974. In 1975 British Leyland sold Innocenti to the De Tomaso Group, who reorganized it as Nuova Innocenti.

NEW ZEALAND

In New Zealand, assembly of ADO16s took place at two separate plants. Austins had traditionally been assembled by Associated Motor Industries in Petone, and so Austin 1100s began to come from that plant in 1963. The Morris link, meanwhile, had traditionally been with Dominion Motors at Newmarket in Auckland, and so Morris 1100 assembly began there in late 1964; some sources claim it actually began as early as 1 February 1963. The two marques maintained the same price hierarchy as in the UK home market, and in 1965 the Morris cost £938 while the Austin cost £945.

As the 1960s progressed, the Newmarket plant also saw the assembly of the MG (by 1964), Riley and Wolseley variants, and by the late 1960s there were 1300 models as well. After a reorganization at the end of the decade, when AMI and Dominion Motors both became part of NZMV (New Zealand

Motor Vehicles), New Zealand imported some Australian-built 1500 models and Nomads, the latter rebadged as Austins!

Broadly speaking, the New Zealand-built version of the standard ADO16s always had the same specifications as the UK models. New Zealand in fact may have been the last country to assemble ADO16s, because the last examples did not leave the New Zealand Motor Corporation plant (the old Dominion Motors plant) in Auckland until April 1976.

SOUTH AFRICA

South Africa began by taking UK-built Morris 1100s in 1962, but the intention was always to proceed to local assembly because of import quota restrictions. Assembly of ADO16s from CKD kits began during 1963 at the BMC plant in Blackheath, Cape Province.

In the beginning there were Austin and MG 1100 saloons, and a Wolseley 1100 was added in late 1966. There was 'still magic in the Wolseley name', noted *Car South Africa* magazine when it tested one in May 1967. The first Wolseleys had the same 55bhp twin-carburettor engine as UK-built models, but in early 1967 the specification was revised and the Wolseley was reintroduced with the 48bhp single-carburettor engine. Austin 1100 Countryman and Morris 1100 Traveller models joined the range in May 1967. All these cars had slightly strengthened body structures to suit South African conditions, and all of them had the uniquely South African feature of a forward-facing white reflector disc on each side of the front panel, between headlamp and side grille.

From January 1968 higher-powered models called the Austin 11/55 and Wolseley 11/55 were introduced. These were so named because they had a 55bhp version of the 1100 (1098cc) engine. However, this engine was not the twin-carburettor type used on UK-built ADO16s. Instead, it had a larger (1.5in) single carburettor, bigger inlet valves, double valve springs and a modified air cleaner.

These versions remained available until 1971, when they were replaced by a new model called the Austin Apache. This was an interesting derivative

of the ADO16, which had started life in the UK as a potential model for overseas markets. Italian stylist Giovanni Michelotti, who had created a number of designs for Triumph in the 1960s, was asked to turn the original two-box ADO16 shape into a three-box design, while retaining the centre body section unchanged. The Michelotti design ended up looking very similar to the Triumph Toledo from some angles, and in fact used the tail lights and outer rear bumper sections from Michelotti's own design for the Triumph 2000 and 2500 cars. Overall, it ended up some 13 inches longer than the original ADO16, with longer front and rear overhangs. Quite what Alec Issigonis made of this adaptation of his original space-saving design seems never to have been recorded.

British Leyland's South African subsidiary, known as Leykor since December 1968, decided to use the Michelotti design as a replacement model for the ADO16. The car was developed jointly between Leyland in Britain and Leykor in South Africa, and went on sale in November 1971. It incorporated some components shipped out from the UK, but was built by the Leyland Car Division at Blackheath in the Cape. These cars had a 1275cc engine developing 62bhp at 5,250rpm, and were available with either manual or automatic transmission. According to *Car South Africa* magazine in December 1971, the manual model accelerated from 0–60mph in 17.2 seconds and had a maximum speed of 88mph. The automatic, tested in the same magazine's April 1972 issue, was a little slower. The 0–60mph time was 18.8 seconds and the maximum speed 83.3mph.

The magazine noted with approval that the boot was now roughly twice as capacious as on the 1100 and 11/55 models, and that the spare wheel could be moved from its vertical mounting at the side to lie flat as a way of increasing maximum width. Less appealing was the retention of the 11/55's strip-type speedometer, albeit enhanced by a wood-grain dashboard finish. A new through-flow ventilation system was a bonus, but its capacity was too low, and the car was much quieter than its predecessors. 'The Apache is a fine achievement by the Leyland organization … Its two chief virtues are its great aesthetic appeal, and its easy-driving

LEFT AND BELOW: **The Austin Apache was an attractive-looking car. The colour picture shows a single-carburettor car that found its way to the UK. The black-and-white picture was a publicity shot of the TC model, which featured Rostyle wheels and a vinyl-covered roof. Note the forward-facing reflectors under the bumpers of both cars, which were a South African requirement. There is a British Leyland badge on the wing of the TC; in South Africa, they were fitted on both sides.**

roadability. It is not an inexpensive car … It is a big advance on the Austin 1100 and 11/55 models.' The automatic 'is a delightful car for commuting, for fetching children from school, for shopping and for the general "get-around" work required of second cars … a serviceable and very attractive light car.'

In 1973 the manual Apache was improved with a more positive gear change that incorporated a rod linkage, and both models gained CV joints instead of the original rubber transmission joints, plus round dials in place of the original strip-type speedometer. At the same time, a twin-carburettor Apache TC became available, with 75bhp at 5,800rpm from its 1275cc engine. Other distinguishing features of this new model were a vinyl roof, a rev counter, a sports steering wheel and Rostyle-pattern wheel trims.

A further model was introduced in May 1976, a limited luxury edition of 300 cars called the Apache

AUSTIN APACHE SALES FIGURES

The following sales figures for the Austin Apache appeared in *Auto Data Digest 1981*, published in 1981 by Mead & McGrouther in Randburg, South Africa.:

	Apache	Apache TC	Total
1971	455		455
1972	3,908		3,908
1973	4,607	649	5,256
1974	3,725	857	4,582
1975	3,356	675	4,031
1976	1,830	517	2,347
1977	749	236	985
1978	49	42	91
Totals	18,679	2,976	21,655

Technical Specifications, Austin Apache

Engine
1300 models
BMC A-series 4-cylinder, with iron block and cylinder
head
1275cc (70.6 × 81.28mm)
Overhead valves; chain-driven camshaft
Three-bearing crankshaft
Compression ratio 9.0:1 (9.1:1 for automatics)
One SU HS4 carburettor
62bhp at 5,250rpm
69 lb ft at 2,500rpm (71 lb ft for automatics)

TC models
BMC A-series 4-cylinder, with iron block and cylinder
head
1275cc (70.6 × 81.28mm)
Overhead valves; chain-driven camshaft
Three-bearing crankshaft
Compression ratio not known
Two SU HS4 carburettors
75bhp at 5,800rpm
Max torque not known

Transmission
Four-speed manual gearbox, with synchromesh on all
forward gears: gear ratios 3.42:1, 2.15:1, 1.387:1, 1.00:1,
reverse 3.44:1
Alternative four-speed AP automatic gearbox: gear
ratios 2.69:1, 1.845:1, 1.48:1, 1,00:1, reverse 2.69:1

Front-wheel drive
Axle ratio
3.76:1

Suspension, steering and brakes
All-round independent suspension with Hydrolastic
units, interconnected front to rear. Front suspension
with wishbones; rear suspension with trailing arms and
anti-roll bar
Rack-and-pinion steering
Front disc brakes and rear drum brakes

Dimensions
Overall length	13ft 2.6in (4,030mm)
Overall width	5ft 0.4in (1,534mm)
Overall height	4ft 4.7in (1,340mm)
Wheelbase	7ft 9.5in (2,375mm)
Front track	4ft 3.5in (1,308mm)
Rear track	4ft 2.9in (1,292mm)

Wheels and tyres
Steel disc wheels
145 × 12 radial tyres

*Licensing mass (South African standard weight
measurement)*
1300 manual	1,863lb (845kg)
1300 automatic	1,905lb (864kg)

35 Special. All were finished in Harvest Gold paint
with a light brown vinyl roof and automatic transmission. They had the Rostyle-pattern wheels and a
special matt black grille with a single chrome strip,
additional stainless steel trim on the flanks, and
unique badges. The seats had brown brushed nylon
upholstery and a brushed nylon trim was used for
the steering wheel spokes, while the carpets were
special in a deep-pile material.

Production of the three mainstream Apache models continued right through into 1978, making them
the last ADO16 derivatives in production anywhere
in the world. More than 21,600 had been built.

SPAIN

In the first half of the 1960s cars imported into
Spain were subjected to very high import taxes,
but the Spanish government was receptive to local
manufacture of foreign vehicles, which would support the local economy. In order to sell cars on
the Spanish market, BMC established Authi as a

joint venture with a Spanish company in 1965. The new assembly plant was located near Pamplona, and its first product was a version of the MG 1100, essentially the standard left-hand-drive model built from CKD. Production began in January 1967 and continued until 1972. Interiors were supposedly supplied by Innocenti in Italy. An Austin 1300 followed, which was conventionally badged but also carried the Authi name at the bottom of the British Leyland wing badge it wore.

Central to the Spanish deal seems to have been a progressive increase in local manufacturing content (a similar arrangement had been made for Land Rover manufacture in Spain). As a follow-up to the MG 1100, Authi picked up on the 1970 'three-box' version of the ADO16 that Michelotti had created for British Leyland and decided to put it into production in Spain. This had the 1275cc engine, and was available from its 1972 launch as an Authi Victoria with a single carburettor and rectangular headlights, or an Authi Victoria De Luxe with 68bhp twin-carburettor engine and twin round headlamps. Unlike the South African-built Austin Apache version of the same design, the Authi Victoria had separate sidelight units mounted above the front bumper.

Authi had further plans, too. At the April 1973 Barcelona Motor Show, the company displayed a prototype MG Victoria. This was a high-performance derivative of the existing Authi Victoria, with MG badges on its grille and Rostyle wheels, and an 83bhp Downton-tuned engine. The car had a sunroof, a brake servo and even air conditioning, with the pump mounted in front of the engine. The interior had also been restyled, with part-cloth seats that had headrests, a wood-rim two-spoke steering wheel, and a padded facia with eyeball vents and a three-dial instrument installation. However, this variant did not enter production, and the best information is that only one other car was built.

Production of the existing Victoria models continued, and Authi came up with a slicker remote-control gear change to improve the cars. This may have been the rod linkage introduced earlier on the South African Austin Apache. From 1974 the Victorias were supplemented by a model simply called the Austin De Luxe. This had the

standard ADO16 four-door body in its Mk III guise, but was intended as an economy model and came with a 55bhp version of the 998cc A-series engine, as used in the Mini at the time. According to the website AROnline, some of these cars were also exported to Denmark and to Greece. However, production was short-lived and ended in 1975.

Meanwhile, a Mk 2 version of the Victoria was being developed, probably for a start to production in late 1974. The Spanish magazine *Cuatro Ruedas* was able to test a prototype of this in its July 1975 issue (and a translation of the article has appeared on the AROnline website). On the outside, the car was distinguished mainly by its fashionable vinyl roof covering and by a slightly altered matt-black grille. A passenger's door mirror was standard, and there was an S on the door pillar where the existing Victoria De Luxe had a V. Inside, it had cloth seats with head restraints, additional soundproofing, and a new dashboard that was similar to the Victoria De Luxe type but now included a trip counter on the speedometer.

There were several mechanical changes. The 1275cc engine now had a 9.5:1 compression ratio and a single SU HS6 carburettor. A new inlet manifold, exhaust system and distributor all contributed to maximum power of 70bhp at 5,750rpm. The radiator had now been moved from the side to the front of the engine bay, and came with an electric cooling fan. There were CV joints in the transmission in place of rubber couplings (again perhaps inspired by the South African example), and a new diaphragm clutch as well. The car was supposedly good for 93mph (150km/h), although the magazine did not attempt to prove that claim.

However, the Mk 2 version did not enter production. A disastrous fire at Authi's Pamplona factory in October 1974 supposedly destroyed stocks of parts for the new model. By this time, British Leyland was running into trouble – it turned to the British government for help at the end of the year – and was unable to provide further support for Authi. The Spanish company struggled on into 1976 but production was halted and the plant was eventually sold to SEAT.

In Spain, the Austin Victoria used twin round headlamps and had sidelights at the body corners, but it was essentially the same car as the Apache. This is a 1973 Victoria Mk II, with vinyl trim on the rear pillars. The rear end with its Triumph saloon lights was common to both models.

CHAPTER EIGHT

BUYING AND OWNING AN ADO16: THE RECKONING

For anybody brought up in the 1960s and 1970s, or for somebody fascinated by that era, an ADO16 must rate very highly as an affordable classic. The cars were an essential part of the British scene at a time before foreign imports had made much of an impact on the preferences of British buyers, and they were much liked. Though never exciting or particularly sporty – not even in 1300GT form – they were practical, comfortable and likeable machines.

Sales figures proved it: more than 2.1 million were sold worldwide and, as noted elsewhere in this book, the ADO16 was the best-selling car in Britain every year from 1963 to 1971, except for 1967. There were multiple variants to suit a variety of different tastes and pockets, and they were for the most part attractively equipped and finished. So why have so few of them survived into the modern era to become cherished classics?

The answer is simple: they rusted as if rusting was going out of fashion. Veteran hands-on motoring journalist Peter Wallage hit the nail right on the head when he wrote in the 5 June 1991 issue of *Autoclassic* magazine that:

The blame must be laid fairly and squarely at the door of the brilliant but autocratic Alec Issigonis … it was typical of the man that he insisted on designing all the structural panels of the car himself instead of leaving it to the far more experienced bodyshell engineers. Though he was an outstanding and visionary mechanical engineer, Issigonis was not a body production engineer.

To be fair, rustproofing was also poorly understood at the time and most British-built cars of the 1960s (and indeed the 1950s and 1970s) suffered badly

All enthusiasts dream of finding a derelict example that is restorable. Unfortunately, the ADO16 range is subject to terminal corrosion and 'barn finds' are likely to consume a lot of time and money to revive – if they can be revived at all.

from corrosion. The ADO16 simply conformed to the rule. But it conformed with frightening speed, and examples were being scrapped in their thousands before they were ten years old.

CHOICES

The remarks that follow on choosing an ADO16 should be tempered with a very heavy dose of realism. Once you have chosen your ideal variant of the ADO16, you may have to spend a very long time looking for one in a condition that is good enough to buy. Above all, do not let your judgement be affected by a pretty colour scheme, an apparently low mileage in a car that has been off the road for many years, or simple nostalgia. With the ADO16, it is not simply a case of throwing money at a car until it is right again (and in any case, you are unlikely ever to recoup that money because resale values have historically always been low). Much more realistic is to consider whether the car can ever be satisfactorily restored at all.

The chapters in this book deliberately divide the varieties of ADO16 up into different types. The everyday family cars came from Austin and Morris, and these two marque badges were also found on the charmingly practical estates. The sporting models came from MG and Riley, although in later years the Austin and Morris 1300GT models also qualified for the category. ('Sporting' of course is a relative term: none of these cars has anything like the performance or handling of a mundane small modern car.) The luxury models came from Wolseley and Vanden Plas.

In the very broadest terms, the rarest of the UK-built cars are those wearing Vanden Plas badges (just 39,471 were made) and Riley badges (just 21,475 were made). Some of the special variants built outside the UK and discussed in Chapter 6 were even rarer, but this guide focuses on those built in the BMC factories at Longbridge and Cowley. If rarity is a factor in desirability, then Riley and Vanden Plas types have to be top of the list. They are, of course, very different cars with very different appeal. As an aside, many really good Vanden Plas survivors were snapped up by collectors in Japan during the 1980s and 1990s, not least because the Japanese have a special affinity for small cars and because these cars combine some very British qualities in their interior trim with that desirable smallness.

Is the bigger-engined 1300 more desirable than the 1100? Realistically, probably not. Although the cars did offer worthwhile performance improvements over their stablemates when they were new, those differences are barely noticeable in modern traffic conditions. Similarly, the slightly less enthusiastic acceleration of ADO16s with automatic transmission is not to be sniffed at today. It really makes very little difference in practical terms because now these cars are, after all, toys to be enjoyed rather than cut-and-thrust road warriors for everyday use. So saying, all of them are perfectly capable of regular road use; they just do not enjoy being rushed.

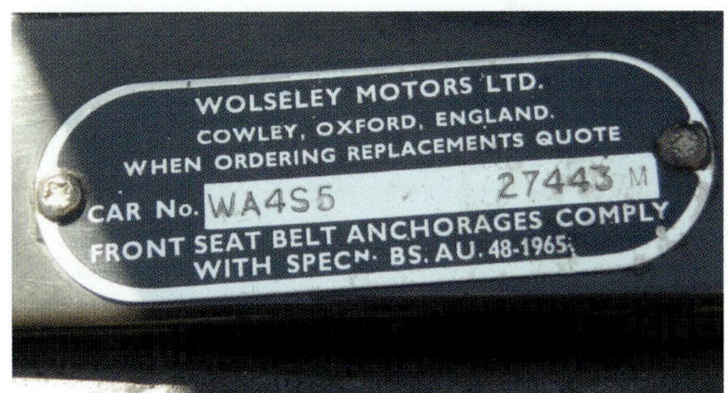

The car's identity is carried on a tag like this, attached to the bonnet slam panel. Reference to the tables in the preceding chapters should identify what it is.

Like all popular cars, the 1100 range attracted aftermarket accessory makers. This boot rack cost £4 19s 6d in August 1963, and was manufactured by Fern Accessories of Coulsdon in Surrey. It would have been ideal for those who thought the boot was too small.

Component manufacturers were rightly proud of their involvement with such a technically advanced car. This was Hardy Spicer's advertisement in *Autocar* for 6 September 1963, the issue that carried news of the Austin 1100's introduction.

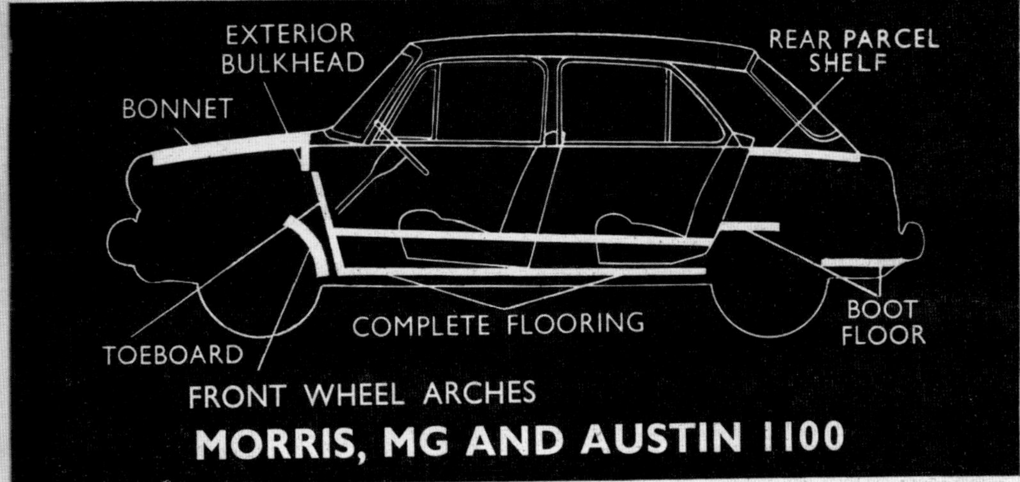

Here was something for those who found the 1100 noisy. Silent Travel soundproofing kits were available for a wide range of popular cars in the 1960s, and it is no surprise that one was made available for the ADO16. For those unfamiliar with the price quoted at the top, '150/-' (150 shillings) equated to £7 10s 0d or £7.50 in modern money.

As for handling, it is good by the standards of the 1960s but may be a surprise to somebody used to driving only more modern cars. The brakes are adequate for modern conditions, but not as good as more modern servo-assisted all-disc systems. As for the ride, it is very good by the standards of the 1960s, although some people have described it as rather choppy and others, strangely, find it induces travel sickness! The sensible thing to do before buying one of these cars is therefore to get some experience of driving one – which, of course, may well be easier said than done.

SUB-FRAME MOUNTINGS

As already explained, the biggest enemy of these cars is rust. A thorough check of the body shell is therefore the most important stage in assessing a potential purchase. It is bodywork that can put an ADO16 beyond repair; mechanical problems can usually be rectified with relatively little difficulty. A car with poor bodywork may not even be worth buying as a source of spares for another one.

Famously, the ADO16 rusts around the mountings of its rear sub-frame. It used to be said (and Peter Wallage recalled this in his *Autoclassic* article mentioned above) that the easy way to change the rear sub-frame on one of these cars was to lift the body up and roll the sub-frame out from underneath. The two really can part company that easily.

As rusted rear sub-frame mountings are the death knell of any ADO16, it is best to start inspection of a car here. The quickest way of getting some idea of its overall condition is to remove the base of the rear seat and to take a look at the rear corners of the seat frame, where the sub-frame bolts can be seen. It will be a rare car that has no rust in the area, but severe rust or holes around the mounting points mean that the car is best left alone. The rest of it will be as bad! If the inside surface of the sub-frame mounting panel looks sound, double-check by looking at it from underneath as well.

The front sub-frame mountings rust, too. To check these, open the bonnet and look at the box-section ahead of the wheel arch on each side. The front sub-frame mountings are here, and it is essential to check the condition of the body shell metal around them from both inside and underneath the car. As with the area of the rear mountings, corrosion here will be difficult or impossible to repair. If things look bad here, it is probably not worth looking at the rest of the car at all.

BODY SHELL UNDERSIDE

If the sub-frame mountings are sound, the next thing to examine is other structural areas of the body shell. As with all monocoque designs, the condition of the body sills is critical, as these provide the strength in the middle of the car. If there is a problem with the door fits, the chances are that the sills have given way and the car is sagging in the middle.

You need to examine the sills from both inside and outside. If the jacking points have collapsed, the sills are rotten and there is no need for a closer inspection. Otherwise, a visual check from outside is easy enough, but it is worth feeling underneath the sills as well, where a little pressure on the metal may reveal corrosion hidden behind the underseal. (This was not applied at the factory, but as it became more popular in the aftermarket during the 1970s, many owners applied it – which was, unfortunately, rather like shutting the stable door after the horse has bolted.)

The next stage is to lift the carpets and take a look at the inner sills from the inside of the car. Look especially around the lower mountings for the seat

Apparently minor problems such as this, on the front end of a sill panel, deserve close investigation. In fact, this is a roughly applied patch of filler and is almost certainly disguising some major corrosion underneath.

belts; experts tell of mountings that pull right out of the sill when given a good hard tug. Then examine the seams between inner sills and floorpan. Holes here spell trouble, and so do holes where the bottom of the toeboard meets the inner front wheel arch. If you are able to take the carpet right out, then do: otherwise, test for corrosion in the floorpan by pressing hard through the carpet and feeling for crumbling metal underneath it. In the days before annual roadworthiness (MoT) testing was as rigorous as it is now, owners used to get away with making patches out of GRP and disguising them with underseal.

If the main floorpan is sound, take a look inside the boot. The boot floor rots along its seam with the rear valance panel, and it is worth examining the spare wheel well and the metal around it, both of which are prone to bad rusting. A particular weak spot is the area where the boot floor meets the inner wings.

Back under the bonnet, there are more areas of metalwork to check. The condition of the seams between inner and outer wings will be immediately obvious. The washer bottle is mounted on a shelf-like structure on the main bulkhead, and corrosion along this shelf is common. If it is very bad, the car is probably best left alone, because repairs in this area can be both tricky and extensive. Engine mountings were a weakness on early cars, and it is advisable to check not only the body metal around them but also the mountings themselves (although, of course, replacing a worn mounting is not a major job). While in the area, it is worth checking the condition of the wiring that passes through the bulkhead. There should be a rubber grommet in place to prevent chafing, but these grommets harden, shrink and fall out, leaving the wiring to rub its insulation away and then short out against the metal bulkhead.

FROM THE OUTSIDE

You will certainly have made an initial assessment of the outer bodywork's condition by this stage, but only now is it worth taking a closer look. There is likely to be rust behind the front bumper, in the seam between the front panel and the lower apron. This can be tricky to repair neatly, but will not put a car off the road. Behind the rear bumper, rot forms a line where the valance joins the vertical rear panel. Once again, it can look bad, but should be repairable.

Front wings rust around the headlamps and down their trailing edges, and they can also rot around the wheel arch lips. Though unsightly, rust in these areas need not be a major cause for concern. A good bodyshop will be able to insert new metal, and a respray will make the wings look as good as new again.

Much the same can be said about the doors. As on most cars of the era, blocked drain holes in the door bottoms will cause water to build up on the inside, where it will eventually promote rust in the bottom of the door skin and even in the bottom of the door frame itself. Really bad cases may be tricky to repair, but in most cases this sort of damage need not be a cause for major concern.

Rust in the rear wheel arches may be more serious, and it is worth checking very carefully for signs of repairs. As in other areas of the body, owners often used to cut out rust and fill the affected area with body filler. That rarely prevented rust from returning, and of course the forward end of the rear wheel arch adjoins the mounting panel for the rear sub-frame, an area already vulnerable enough to rusting of its own accord. It was a rare owner who went to the expense of having the job done properly by a bodyshop, and getting the rust cut out and replaced by new metalwork.

INTERIOR

The condition of the interior is easy to assess, and the good news is that this area of the ADO16 usually wore well. Early seat coverings often respond well to a good clean, although there is little to be done with the later vacuum-formed vinyl coverings if they have dried out and cracked. A particular problem to look out for on Mk III models is a cracked dashboard.

Most important to remember is that replacement interior trim is now more or less non-existent. The days when parts could be found in every scrapyard are now many years in the past, and owners may have to resort to such things as lambswool seat covers until good replacement seats turn up.

When the cars were new, tall drivers often complained that the driving position allowed them

Leather upholstery was an extra-cost option on the Austin 1100 when it was announced in 1963. Today, it is a desirable find – and probably easier to replace than the original standard upholstery material.

insufficient legroom. This was easily rectified (and obviously can be today as well) by reversing the retaining brackets for the seat, which gives another couple of inches for the driver.

ENGINES

By comparison with the structure of the car, the engine is likely to give only minor cause for concern. Generally speaking, the BMC A-series is a very durable unit and it will keep going even when suffering from a variety of maladies. Its simple and robust design means it is not difficult to overhaul for the keen DIY enthusiast, and there are plenty of knowledgeable specialists around, while spare parts are not a problem on the whole.

It loses oil, of course. If it is not obvious where the oil is going, then the probability is that it is being drawn up the bores and puffed out through the exhaust. In bad cases, this will be obvious as a blue haze in the exhaust, but quite a lot of oil can disappear before the telltale sign becomes unmistakeable. In fact, the A-series engine regularly consumed a pint in every 500 miles or less when it was new. Much more obvious than oil loss in this fashion is an oil leak through the timing cover seal; not only will there be oil on the outside of the engine, but sooner or later a puddle on the ground below the car as well. A leak from the drain hole under the clutch housing is probably the result of a failed rear main bearing seal.

High-mileage engines, or those that have not been well maintained, often have very rattly timing chains. A proper overhaul is the most sensible course of action. Rocker shafts wear and need replacing as the miles mount up. On the twin-carburettor engines, balancing the carburettors is now seen as a tricky job because few people are familiar with what is needed in an age of fuel injection and electronic control systems. In practice, balancing carburettors is not at all difficult – although a specialist may be needed to deal with cases of wear that prevent a satisfactory balance from being achieved.

Worth knowing is that the additional power and taller gearing of the 1300 models make these cars more relaxed at speed and generally less noisy than the 1100s that preceded them.

A typically neglected engine bay, in this case in a late Austin that has not been used for some time. There are oil leaks and rust everywhere, and several rubber grommets have been displaced or are missing – but it can probably be persuaded to run with a new battery and a bit of effort.

GEARBOX AND DRIVE SHAFTS

All the BMC gearbox-in-sump manual gearboxes have a characteristic whine that is nothing to cause concern. Similarly, first gear is often hard to engage from neutral when the gearbox is cold, and the usual 'fix' is simply to dab the clutch twice before moving the selector lever. However, if gear selection is generally difficult, or if the gearbox sounds generally harsh, then it is likely that the gearbox centre bearing is excessively worn. This can be replaced fairly easily.

A rattling noise from the gearbox when the engine is idling often comes from a worn idler gear, which transfers the drive from the end of the crankshaft to the gearbox. Again, this is not an insuperable problem, but it is more time-consuming as a repair because the engine bell-housing has to be removed in order to gain access. As many cars had this rattle from new, the time to worry is when and if the noise gets worse.

The AP automatic gearboxes are reasonably trouble-free, although it appears that US owners had a lot of trouble with them in Austin America models. This might have resulted from unfamiliarity with the characteristics of the transmission: when the lever is in '3', for example, the transmission is locked in third gear and will not shift down to 2 and 1 like a more conventional automatic. Acceleration improvements can be made by adjusting the kick-down rod to raise the speed at which the transmission kicks down, so keeping the engine in its power band for longer.

The drive shaft couplings will fail after time, but without serious consequences. The usual warning sign is a loud clicking noise from the failed joint, and that noise becomes louder if the car is accelerated fairly hard from standstill with the steering on full lock.

SUSPENSION

The concept of the Hydrolastic suspension frightens some people, but the system is actually relatively simple and rarely gives trouble. Pipes can fracture and leak, of course, but the original steel items can now be replaced with modern plastic types that are not vulnerable to corrosion. Some cars may ride higher on one side than on the other, but this problem is simply fixed by adjusting the suspension pressure – not a DIY job, incidentally, because of the high pressures at which the system works. Other imbalances can usually be cured by having the system drained, flushed through and refilled to the original specification. Obviously, it is also possible for a leak to cause complete collapse of the suspension on one side, a fault that is immediately obvious.

Some cars also suffer from failure of the pivot bearings in the rear trailing arms. This can be detected by lifting each rear wheel clear of the ground (the car must be jacked under the body, not under the suspension arm itself) and checking for movement.

The suspension units are not normally as visible as this one, which is seen in the cutaway display Austin Countryman built in 1966.

INDEX